Sack your Financial Adviser

How to take control and build wealth on your terms

Adem Becirevic

First published 2026 by Adem Becirevic
www.virtualfinancial.com.au

Produced by Independent Ink

Cover design by Catucci Design
Edited by Lucy Czerwinski
Internal design by Independent Ink
Typeset in Gotham by Post Pre-press Group, Brisbane
Cover image: Dragon Claws/istockphoto.com

NATIONAL LIBRARY OF AUSTRALIA

A catalogue record for this book is available from the National Library of Australia

ISBN 978-1-7647800-0-1 (paperback)
ISBN 978-1-7647800-1-8 (epub)
ISBN 978-1-7647800-2-5 (kindle)

I would like to dedicate this book to my wife who has always encouraged to share my experiences and has been very patient whilst writing the book, to professionals like Gary Weigh who has given so much to the industry. To my team at Virtual Financial that keep me going and push to be my best. To Rob Coyte the CEO of my dealer group Shartru Wealth who has been a great help with his MDA's. To Ann Dettori from Dettori Publishing who has been very patient, this book would not be possible without her efforts. To Colin Lee who helped write the section on property, he is a wealth of knowledge. And to everyone that has supported me including my clients who are all like family to me.

Contents

Introduction

Hi, I'm Adem (pronounced Adam) and I'm a financial adviser. I would like to start by saying that I understand. I understand the worries that might be keeping you up at night. I understand that fear of the unknown that can come with planning for your financial future and retirement. It can be easy to procrastinate and put your financial wellbeing in the too-hard basket. Do not worry, you are not alone.

In fact, a surprising number of Australians share these feelings. According to a recent study, over half of Australians do not feel adequately prepared for retirement.[1] They, like you, are on the search for clarity, guidance and a sense of control over their financial future.

Retirement planning isn't only about how much money you have. It's about understanding what you want your retirement to look like. People in their twenties will have a very different viewpoint to those in their forties and fifties. Planning needs to take into consideration your life at the present, what your goals are and how you can best position yourself to achieve this.

For a moment, imagine the peace of mind you will have if you are able to take control of your finances with the right advice. The certainty that you will have, the feeling that you are making the right decisions and the confidence you will have. Now, here is the good news: you do not need to do it alone. With the right financial adviser by your side, that peace of mind and certainty can be yours. No more sleepless nights worrying about the future.

Your relationship with money

We all have a unique relationship with money. This has been influenced by our upbringing, our experiences and our personal values. My personal relationship with money has been influenced by my family and the challenges my parents faced when I was growing up. I can look back on those times and now see how this has shaped my financial journey. It taught me to work hard and to save for my first home deposit. Seeing my parents struggle to buy their first home really gave me the motivation to ensure that I prioritised saving for that deposit. This relationship with money is especially important to keep in mind when setting financial goals with your spouse as you will both have a unique relationship with your finances that will impact your approach. These experiences and values shape our financial habits, and by extension, our financial future. To effectively plan your financial journey, we need to understand and acknowledge this relationship.

I want to stress here that there is no 'one-size-fits-all' solution to financial planning. Every individual, every couple, every family has unique circumstances, needs and desires. And the plan should reflect your individuality, not what you think a financial plan should look like. Just as a doctor wouldn't prescribe medication without understanding your symptoms, a financial adviser shouldn't provide advice without understanding your life circumstances.

The importance of a good financial adviser

The title of this book might sound odd for a book written by a financial adviser, but I firmly believe that if you are working with an adviser who does not set you up for success then it might be time to find someone who will. But how do you know what a good retirement plan that meets your needs looks like and what are the right questions to ask? This is where I can help.

Firstly, why is seeing a financial adviser so important?

Personalised guidance: Your financial adviser should help align your finances with your life goals, making sure your money is working as hard as you are.

Accountability: They can keep you on track, helping you stay disciplined about your financial strategies. They are like a coach: someone who can challenge you whilst also being on your team.

Peace of mind: You can sleep at night knowing that you have a plan in place for your financial future that will cover you if something unexpected happens. You will have peace of mind knowing that you and your family will be okay.

As I have said and will say throughout the book, it is not just about seeing a financial adviser; it's about finding the right one for you. Like all professions, there are good ones and bad ones. I found this out when I renovated my house. There are definitely good builders and bad builders.

The saying at Virtual Financial Advice is that it starts with you. I believe no one is going to help you, so you must take the initiative and help yourself. Using our questionnaires makes it very easy to start this process. Head to our website to complete the financial health check: **www.virtualfinancial.com.au**

The financial industry and its challenges

I've spent years in the Australian financial industry, initially as an accountant before transitioning into financial planning. I'm proud to say that I am now a Fellow Certified Practicing Accountant (FCPA) with the highest standing within this industry.

During my career, I have seen ups and downs in the industry and my experience has led me to understand the challenges that can arise. I have seen how excessive paperwork, compliance and government intervention can make financial planning a daunting task for many. The system, as it is, often leads to high costs for clients and an absence of affordable, quality advice. We need to change this, and it starts with empowering you, the client.

Let's do this together

This book isn't just about how to manage your money; it is so much more. It's about understanding why you make the decisions you do, and how those decisions affect your financial health, which can affect your mental and physical health. It's about setting clear goals and making a plan to achieve them. It's about having the right support along the way.

In the following pages, I hope to provide you with the tools you need to take control of your financial future. I want to help you understand the importance of getting the right advice and how to recognise when you're not getting it. I want to demystify the financial jargon that stands as a barrier between you and your money.

I will also outline how you can minimise risk by taking out the right insurance for you, and the impact this can have on you and your family's financial wellbeing if you get this wrong. I will also look at superannuation and the benefits that go with carefully planning the right structure and investments. You have no doubt heard the saying, 'you don't know, what you don't know' so the sooner you learn, the sooner you can make changes.

So, let's do this together. Let's take charge of your financial future and determine your goals. Let's plan for a retirement that doesn't just meet your needs but truly fulfils your aspirations.

PART ONE

It's All in the Planning

How Family History Impacts Your Relationship with Money

Before we dive deeper into the world of financial planning, I'd like to share a bit about my own journey, about the humble beginnings that shaped my relationship with money. You might see some similarities in your own story, or it may be entirely different. Either way, understanding our past helps us build a better future.

My story

Like many in this diverse country of ours, my family's journey to Australia wasn't a simple one. My father, like so many, escaped from Bosnia after the carnage of World War II with hopes and dreams for a better future packed alongside his survival instincts. He worked arduously in Italy, saving every penny, every lira, to eventually venture to the land down under and build a new life for himself.

On reaching the shores of New South Wales, Dad found employment in the Snowy Mountains and later the Hydro Scheme. His work also took him to the underground tunnels in Sydney, a city where we lived for a number of years. Meeting my mother, a nurse freshly arrived from the UK, was another beautiful chapter in his life.

As first-generation immigrants, they didn't have an extended family network here. It was just us. And yes, there were moments of loneliness, times when we lived in housing commission homes and periods of financial strain.

But here's the thing. I grew up with a determination to better myself, as did my brother and sisters. Observing my parents navigate through their challenges, making wise choices even in scarcity, sparked something in me. It led me to a career in accounting, and then, financial planning.

The ambition to excel didn't stop there. I found myself setting up my own business, and today I am a proud FCPA that specialises in financial advice.

My passion for finance and property came in handy when I was able to help my parents purchase their first home. This modest investment turned out to be the turning point for them. As the property value increased substantially over the years, allowing them the opportunity to sell at the right time and thus funding their comfortable retirement on the Gold Coast. I am very proud of my part in helping ensure they can enjoy their retirement and not worry about paying the bills.

Lessons from my childhood

Growing up, money was tight in our home. My father and mother worked relentlessly to provide for us, but the returns on manual labour weren't high back in those days. We learned to value every dollar, even the small joy of fish-and-chips for less than a dollar was something to look forward to and not take for granted.

These experiences didn't just influence my career choice; they shaped my ethos. They taught me to work hard, to appreciate the things I have, to extend kindness, and to help others. My siblings and I took these lessons to heart, and they've guided our lives.

Your relationship with money

Now, let's turn the spotlight on you. Your family, like mine, may have played a significant role in shaping your relationship with money. Perhaps your parents were risk-averse or maybe they embraced financial risks. Either way, their approach would have influenced your own relationship with money.

It's important to note that there's no right or wrong relationship with money. It's simply different for each person and made up of your unique set of values and goals. Your money mindset, which could be a direct result of your upbringing, plays a key role in your financial decisions today. I'm not going to preach to you to do a budget and watch every dollar. I think that's a recipe for disaster. When you don't stick to your budget, it can have a bad effect on your mental health. I believe in setting goals and being disciplined with your efforts. Like training for a marathon, you must be consistent but not let setbacks stop you from achieving your goals.

Reflecting on the past

If you struggle with managing your finances or feel uncertain for your retirement, it's worth delving into your past. Consider the financial attitudes you observed growing up. Reflect on how these experiences might have influenced your financial habits today. Understanding this connection can be the first step towards taking control of your financial future and being happy with the relationship you have with money.

The road ahead

My parent's journey, their struggle and their resilience, has been my inspiration. It has been my compass as I navigate the world of financial planning, helping others understand and manage their relationship with money.

In the chapters ahead, I will guide you to take control of your financial future. No jargon, no complex strategies, just practical and personalised advice.

Remember, your relationship with money is just that – yours. It is unique, personal and ever evolving. And just like any relationship, it's something that can be understood, nurtured and developed for the better.

The Importance of Financial Advice

In life, uncertainty is a given. This is especially true for personal finances if you don't have a plan and goals in place. Regardless of your current circumstances or the financial values you've inherited from your family, it's always wise to consult a financial adviser (also known as a financial planner). Even if you think you have a handle on your financial situation, it's beneficial to get a second opinion. Why? Because everyone's circumstances and goals are different and they change over time.

Six steps to financial freedom

At Virtual Financial Advice we help our clients understand their financial future using the following blueprint. If you adapt the same strategies, you will be on your way to financial certainty.

1. **Annual financial health day**: Dedicate one day each year to review and calculate your financial health, this is done by yourself or with your partner at a cafe or somewhere you can relax

and discuss your financial health. Some like to do this in June to coincide with the end of financial year, others may do this when their yearly review is due.

2. **Do a retirement plan**: It's amazing how many clients I meet that do not have one. Most clients don't realise they may be on track for a comfortable retirement.

3. **Financial Health questionnaire**: Our questionnaire is designed to delve into six key areas of your financial life. By filling this out, you'll gain an understanding of whether you are on track in each area or if you have work to do. This is on the home page of our website: **www.virtualfinancial.com.au**.

4. **Personalised financial advice**: Seek out a qualified financial adviser who listens and provides personalised advice on your situation, not a one-size-fits-all solution. You don't know what you don't know.

5. **Compound interest and investing:** Be consistent and remember the rule of 72. Your return divided by 72 tells you how often you will double your money. This is a rule of thumb.

6. **It starts with you**, no one is going to save you. Do the questionnaires and follow the steps in this book.

Following these steps can help you retire early, wealthy and with the freedom to choose your lifestyle. However, achieving financial freedom requires careful planning and strategies. The amount of money you need to live on now may be vastly different in the decades to come. This is why I wrote this book – to guide you through various life stages and help you navigate the path to financial freedom, no matter what your current situation is.

The importance of financial education

Unfortunately, many of us are not taught these valuable lessons when we are young. I believe the education system is failing our children by not teaching financial literacy from a young age. Life can take unexpected turns, like death, divorce or illness, which can drastically affect our financial planning and lifestyle. Understanding how to navigate these changes and adjust your goals is essential.

Case studies: learn from real-life examples

To illustrate how versatile financial planning can be, I'll introduce you to six real-life examples. These case studies, based on a combination of my clients' experiences, will be woven throughout this book. Each of them has a unique financial journey, but their desire to work with a financial adviser is a common thread, as is their desire for a secure retirement. You might even see yourself or someone you know in these stories.

Let's meet our case studies

Under 40s

Kieran (26) and Caitlin (28)

Current situation: Currently renting and plan to purchase a townhouse.

Concerns: Affording a wedding and a mortgage in an expensive property market.

Goals: To get married, have children and create wealth.

Hobbies: Basketball, gym, golf and running.

Nick (35) and Talisha (34)

Current situation: Married with one child and own a small house.

Concerns: Upgrading their home and understanding how to buy property using their superannuation.

Goals: To buy an investment property.

Hobbies: Mountain biking and running an online business.

Joe (37) and Matt (38)

Current situation: High income with no kids and own an apartment.

Concerns: Setting up a low-risk investment plan with superannuation.

Goals: To retire at 60.

Hobbies: Eating out, travel and photography.

40s

Shane (40) and Kristal (39)

Current situation: Shane is a dentist with a business and 8 staff, and Kristal works as a receptionist. Considering an investment property to create wealth.

Concerns: Low super as Shane has used most of his funds for his business.

Goals: To pay off home loan before retirement. To retire at 63 and 62. Once accumulated enough super balance, would like to consider a self-managed super fund (SMSF) and buy dental practice.

Karen (42)

Current situation: Small mortgage.

Concerns: Upgrading her house or purchasing an investment property. Not confident with finances and concerned about retirement.

Goals: To set up an investment plan.
Hobbies: Shopping and competitive dancing.

50s

<u>**Ant (57) and Emily (56)**</u>
Current situation: Previously married, with 7 children between them and own a small business.
Concerns: Funding retirement, investing business proceeds into super.
Goals: To retire at 70 (Ant) and 67 (Emily) and spend time in the UK.
Hobbies: Renovating their home and spending time with their grandkids.

60s

<u>**Warren (67) and Victoria (67)**</u>
Current situation: Recently retired with $400,000 each in super.
Concerns: Ensuring their retirement savings last for a comfortable lifestyle.
Goals: To travel extensively in the first few years of their retirement.
Hobbies: Spending time with their grandkids.

As we journey through this book, we'll follow these real-life examples and learn how they navigate their financial futures with confidence. No matter where you are in life, their stories will show you that it's never too late or too early to start planning your financial freedom.

Understanding Key Terms

In the introduction I assured you this was not going to be a book filled with industry jargon, but it is important to understand the key terms and phrases we use. This allows you to have a meaningful conversation with your financial adviser without needing to have a finance degree. It gives you the knowledge to understand what questions you need to ask and what you need to learn more about.

First up we are going to look at my favourite planning tool, superannuation.

Superannuation

Let's begin by breaking down super into everyday language. Think of superannuation as your personal money pot for retirement. It's there to provide you with an income when you decide to say goodbye to the workforce.

On 1st July 1992, the Australian Government came up with a system called the Superannuation Guarantee (SG). Simply put, the SG is a rule mandates that your employer must put a portion of your salary into your superannuation fund. This was originally set at 3% and is now 12% of your gross income.

There are five main types of superannuation investment options to choose from:

1. **Retail superannuation:** These are usually run by banks or investment companies.

2. **Corporate superannuation**: If you're part of a specific corporate organisation, you might have one of these.

3. **Industry superannuation:** These funds are typically linked to specific industries but are often open to anyone to join and can be union-based funds.

4. **Self-managed super fund (SMSF):** Managing your own super, but it does come with a lot of responsibility.[2]

5. **Government superannuation:** These funds are for people who work in the public sector.

Common industry jargon

Asset: Anything of value that you own. Assets can be physical (like a house or investment property) or non-physical (like shares and bonds).

Liability: Any money that you owe to someone else, including loans, credit card debt or a mortgage.

Equity: In the context of real estate, equity is the market value of a property minus any mortgage owed on it. In terms of investments, equity can also refer to shares owned in a company.

Diversification: Spreading your investments across different types of asset classes (like shares, bonds, property, crypto and cash) to reduce risk.

Portfolio: The total collection of your investments, such as shares, bonds, cash and property.

Risk Tolerance: Your ability and willingness to lose some or all of your original investment in exchange for greater potential returns.

Liquidity: How quickly and easily and asset can be converted into cash.

Inflation: The rate at which the general level of prices for goods and services is rising and subsequently the rate that purchasing power is falling.

Capital gain: The profit made from the sale of an asset, like property or shares, when you sell it for more than you paid for it.

Compound interest: Interest calculated on the initial principal and on the accumulated interest of previous periods of a deposit or loan.

Annuity: A financial product, typically sold by a life insurance company, that guarantees regular payments over a certain period in exchange for an upfront investment.

Estate planning: The process of anticipating and arranging for the disposal of an estate (all the things you own) during your life. Estate planning typically includes planning for incapacity as well as eliminating uncertainties over the administration of your estate. This includes an up-to-date will and Enduring Power of Attorney.

Managed discretionary account (MDA): A type of investment service in Australian finance where a client entrusts an investment manager with the discretion to make investment decisions on their behalf. This means that the manager has the authority to buy and sell securities in the client's account without seeking approval for each transaction. The investment strategy is guided by a pre-agreed investment program based on the client's investment objectives, financial situation and needs. The benefits of an MDA include personalised management of your portfolio, potentially quicker investment decisions and access to investment opportunities that might not otherwise be available to individual investors.

Separately managed accounts (SMA): A portfolio of assets managed by a professional investment manager mainly used by retail super and industry funds on behalf of individuals and investors, unlike managed funds where the investment manager makes investment decisions on behalf of the investors, SMA is a more personalised investment portfolio.

Managed funds: Professionally managed investment vehicle that pools funds from multiple investors and invests the funds based on the fund's objectives and strategies.

Transfer balance cap: A limit placed on the total amount of super you can transfer into tax-free retirement income streams during the retirement phase of superannuation.

• • •

Meeting with a financial adviser for the first time might feel daunting. You might be unsure of where to start, what information you'll need to share, or how to identify which options are best for you, especially when it comes to superannuation. But don't worry, I can help. I will shed light on what you can expect when working with a financial planner and dispel any myths about an industry I've been part of for more than 30 years.

I've had conversations with millionaires as well as thousands of people who are living pay cheque to pay cheque. I've met young adults with trust funds, and others weighed down by university debts and dreams that feel out of reach.

But here's the truth: for everyone, no matter where they are on their financial journey, nothing is impossible. All it takes to pave the path to financial freedom is a bit of money, strategic planning and the determination to see it through.

What Do You Need Before You Start?

Who are you, where are you and what got you to this point? These are often the first things a financial planner will want to know about you. As we have already discovered, there are many similarities in the types of people who seek advice from a financial adviser, and just as it is for someone seeking medical help, the more that's understood about the patient's situation, the easier it is to prescribe the right treatment. When you see a doctor, the first thing they will do is ask questions and take your blood pressure to form a basis for their diagnosis for your medical problems. I was once at a conference on the Gold Coast where the head of the Australian Medical Association said, 'If your doctor doesn't take your blood pressure, then you should change doctors.' Blood pressure gives the doctor a good indication on what's going on with your body, and when it comes to financial advice, if your current provider is not 'taking your blood pressure', that is, not creating a retirement plan, I would recommend changing advisers.

No matter how much money you have, what your age is or what your job is like, it's crucial to know where you stand financially. And it's just as important to be prepared for life's unexpected turns. The best way to deal with surprises? Have a good plan in place.

Now is a great time to sit down with your partner if you have one, or just with yourself, and ask where you sit on these situations:

- Do you have dependents (like parents and children) who need your support?
- Are you satisfied with your job and have good job security?
- Is your current home a good fit for your long-term needs?
- What are the priorities on your bucket list?
- What are your goals?

Knowing where you stand on these five areas will help you get the most out of your meeting with a financial adviser and will help them get a clearer picture of who you are and where you are heading. It also helps you work out if you and your partner are on the same page when it comes to these topics. Are there any disagreements that need to be discussed? Now is a great time to work on common goals and see where you can compromise on others.

• • •

To help you prepare, I've created a checklist that has been divided into six key areas. Some of the questions might not apply to you, and that's okay. This is just a starting point to get you thinking.

When working with our clients we find it is not uncommon for one partner to take the lead in managing household finances. This can occur for various reasons such as traditional gender roles, differences in interest or expertise or the division of labour within the relationship.

No matter what the reason for this, I recommend that both partners be involved in the financial decision-making to some extent. Even if only one person is doing the day-to-day heavy lifting it is important for both parties to understand where their money is and what the overall financial plan/goal is.

This is important for several reasons:

- **Knowledge and understanding:** Both partners having a good understanding of the family's finances can lead to better financial decision-making. They can support each other and provide a second opinion on matters.
- **Risk management:** If the partner who usually handles the finances becomes ill, incapacitated or passes away, the other partner may be left in a difficult situation if they do not understand their financial situation. This is not an uncommon situation in older couples, where one spouse dies and the other has little to no understanding of their finances.
- **Empowerment and equality:** Financial literacy can lead to a sense of empowerment and equality in a relationship, potentially reducing conflicts that can arise due to financial matters.
- **Planning for the future:** Both partners need to be involved in planning for their combined future, this includes retirement planning, since these decisions will affect both individuals.

It might feel easier and timesaving to have one partner take on the lion's share of the financial responsibilities, but it is beneficial for both partners in a relationship to have an understanding of their unique situation and be involved in the decision-making.

Don't put this off, sit down with your partner (if you have one), grab a cup of tea (or a glass of wine) and a pen. Start by ticking the boxes you are confident you can answer a yes to; leave blank the ones that are a no or you are only partially confident on. (You can also find this checklist on our website at no cost.) The Financial Health check can be completed online at **www.virtualfinancial.com.au**.

Income plan

- ○ My current income meets my living costs
- ○ My income is well structured and tax efficient
- ○ My children's education costs are covered
- ○ Surplus income is being invested for wealth creation
- ○ My employment is secure

Investment plan

- ○ I have an appropriate 5-year wealth plan
- ○ I have investment setup to reduce tax efficiently
- ○ I understand my current investment strategy and the risks
- ○ My investments are achieving my goals
- ○ I can sleep at night with current investments that are in place

Debt plan

- ○ My debt is structured in the best possible way
- ○ I have right mix of personal and investment debt
- ○ I have a plan to eliminate personal debt as soon as possible
- ○ Debt levels are appropriate for my current life status
- ○ My debt plan is reviewed yearly

Risk plan

- ○ My insurances cover me comprehensively for most foreseeable circumstances
- ○ I am paying the most competitive premiums
- ○ I have the appropriate levels of cover in place
- ○ My family would continue to live comfortably if something happened to me
- ○ My insurance policies are reviewed each year

Retirement plan

- ○ I have a clear understanding of my retirement goals
- ○ I have a clear understanding of my income required in retirement
- ○ I am on track to achieve my required income in retirement
- ○ My retirement funds will last throughout my retirement
- ○ My retirement strategy is structured tax efficiently

Estate plan

- ○ My will is up to date and reflects my current wishes
- ○ My assets will be transferred to all the right people at the right time tax efficiently
- ○ I have someone to make financial decisions on my behalf if I am unable to do so
- ○ My surviving family members or executor would easily find all relevant documentation
- ○ My family is aware of my medical and lifestyle wishes

• • •

Add up your numbers – giving one point for each answer you have ticked as a yes.

22–30: you seem to have everything well sorted. Keep going.

12–22: You will benefit from having a conversation with a financial adviser and continue working progressively towards getting your finances in the best shape they can be.

Fewer than 11: You really need to spend some time on this, and a great place to start is by continuing reading.

As you can see this is a comprehensive list and includes much more than your superannuation savings.

The goal is to get your score to 30, and that would then mean you have everything under control and are on track. We work with you towards getting you to 100% on the Financial Health check.

When planning for the future it is important to look at the big picture, not just your superannuation. Completing this checklist will help you see the broader perspective and hopefully get you thinking about things that haven't occurred to you. Whether you're just starting out, growing your family or thinking about retirement, a good financial plan will help make your dreams a reality.

If we look at the stages each of our real-life examples are at, we can get an idea of how everyone's plan is different, but the desired outcome is similar; to retire comfortably with a secure ongoing income no matter what life throws at us.

Real Life Examples

Kieran and Caitlin are starting out on their financial journey but are living in very different times to their parents. Property prices are on the rise and many fear home ownership is simply a pipe dream.

Nick and Talisha are in their thirties, have a child and dream of a bigger home. They don't have much time for anything other than work, and their spare income goes towards paying down their mortgage to get ahead by the time they are forty. Their needs are quite diverse compared to that of our other case studies. They are also in the statistical group where divorce is higher, career change is greater, and they may not have finished having children yet. Their need for income protection insurance and to have a plan for 'what if' is just as big a need as ensuring the mortgage is paid and their lifestyle is healthy at this stage of their lives.

Joe and Mark are in a very different situation all together. They have high incomes and have no plans to start a family, but that does not mean it is all smooth sailing for them. It is not uncommon for Australians to live beyond their means and save little more than the government mandated super guarantee, leaving them not much better off than someone who started planning early, on less income.

Karen on the other hand, has no commitments, no dependents, a job she could continue to do for as long as she wants to, or she could change and do something else in the next 20–30 years. She has many options, owns her apartment and has some ability to invest further in something that expands her choices in the years to come.

On the other hand, **Ant and Emily** have put a lot of funds into their business so how do they ensure they will be okay in retirement? How do they get funds into super as they now have contribution limits, and how do they sell the business and the surgery and optimise their super balances?

Wayne and Victoria have already retired. They have started to live on their combined super funds and want to be sure that they are not going to run out of money in another 15 years if they do the things they always wanted to do at this stage in their lives. They would love to travel for a year, hike parts of Europe and scuba dive in Mexico while they're still fit and healthy. But how much should they spend for that dream, and what compromises must they consider if they expand the travel budget? How do they maximise what funds they have?

Are you protected against potential risks? Do you have income protection, life insurance or trauma insurance in place? If unsure, we have a comprehensive checklist on our website that can help you navigate these areas. And we will delve into each of these topics in more detail in the following chapters.

Remember, the journey to financial wellness begins with understanding where you are starting from. It's about knowing what you need, what you have and what steps you need to take to achieve your financial goals.

If you haven't already completed the checklist, go back and do that before reading on.

Your First Meeting with a Financial Adviser: What to Expect and How to Prepare

Stepping into a financial adviser's office or meeting virtually for the first time might feel a bit overwhelming, but it needn't be. It's an essential step on your path to financial stability and retirement readiness. With a little preparation, you can make the most out of this initial meeting and set a solid foundation for your future financial planning.

Understanding your current situation

The first part of the meeting will likely revolve around understanding your current situation. A great place to start is by completing the checklist in the previous chapter and if you haven't already done that, I suggest now is a great time to put down this book and complete it.

There are common questions your financial adviser will ask you:

Personal information: This includes your age, family status, health status and occupation. These details allow your adviser to gain a comprehensive view of your lifestyle, obligations and potential future needs. For example, having young children may necessitate plans for future education expenses.

Financial position: You'll be asked to provide information about your income, expenses, assets and liabilities. These insights will help your adviser assess your current financial health, and they form the baseline from which your financial plan will evolve. Be ready with specifics, as they'll allow your adviser to craft the most effective strategy for you. Now is not the time to sugar coat your levels of debt or spending habits, remember it is not the adviser's role to judge you but to help you to determine a plan that will work for you and your goals.

Existing insurance policies: Your adviser will need details of any existing insurance policies and their coverage. This information is crucial for identifying any gaps in your coverage and ensuring that you and your loved ones are adequately protected in the event of unexpected occurrences.

Superannuation and other retirement savings: The details of your superannuation funds, as well as any other retirement savings or pension schemes you're part of, will be crucial in planning for your retirement. They can significantly inform how much more you need to save and the best strategies to do so.

Current investment portfolio: If you've already started investing, your adviser will want to review your current portfolio. They can evaluate its performance, risk level and alignment with your goals.

Goals and objectives

Your financial adviser will also need to understand your life goals. These goals will form the roadmap for your financial plan:

Short-term goals (1–5 years): These could include plans like purchasing a new car, travelling or saving up for a major life event. Knowing these objectives allows your adviser to allocate funds and manage your cash flow appropriately.

Medium-term goals (5–15 years): Medium-term goals might involve funding your children's education, upgrading your properties, paying off your mortgage or maybe starting a small business. These goals affect how your adviser will strategise your investment and savings plan.

Long-term goals (15+ years): Long-term goals often revolve around retirement planning and estate planning. These are big-picture goals that need time and careful planning to achieve. Identifying these early on will guide your financial plan's overall direction.

Determining what these goals are will be individual to you and what stage of life you are at. There is no right or wrong way to set these goals, and it is very helpful to have an idea of what you want to achieve before meeting with your adviser.

Examples of goals may include:

- Buying your first home
- Paying off your mortgage
- Buying an investment property
- Paying off credit card debt
- Going on an overseas trip

- Paying less tax
- Starting a share portfolio
- Helping your kids buy their first home
- Retiring with $1,000,000

Risk profiling

Finally, a vital part of the initial meeting will be understanding your tolerance for risk. This assessment is crucial for creating an investment strategy that you're comfortable with, and as previously discussed, this can be influenced by your upbringing. A great place to start is to sit down with your partner and discuss the following:

Evaluating your risk tolerance: Most financial advisers will use a combination of questionnaires and discussions to understand your comfort level with risk. Be honest during this process. It's essential that any plan developed aligns with your risk tolerance, so you can stick with it in the long run. At my practice we ask a series of questions ensuring you understand the risk-return trade-off, and the importance of getting this right. Having the wrong profile can really affect your retirement. I have seen clients who have been with industry funds, and their profile has been conservative over a long period. As a result, they were missing great returns in the market as they did not get advice and unfortunately could not retire comfortably.

Understanding your previous investment experience: Your adviser will ask about your past experiences with investments, both positive and negative. This conversation can offer valuable insights into your investment behaviour and preferences. This is especially important when working as a couple.

Discussing trade-offs between risk and return: Your adviser will likely discuss the trade-offs between risk and return with you. Understanding your willingness to accept risk for potential returns helps tailor an investment strategy that fits you best.

The first meeting with a financial adviser is all about getting to know you, your current financial status, your future goals and your risk tolerance. The best way to prepare is to complete 2 questionnaires: the Financial Health check and the All About You questionnaire. Think carefully about your short, medium and long-term goals, and reflect on your comfort with risk. Remember, this meeting is your stepping stone to a more secure financial future and a comfortable retirement. Be open and honest, and together, you can craft a financial plan that aligns with your aspirations and lifestyle.

PART TWO

The Ins and Outs of Superannuation

Superannuation: What you need to know

Anyone who knows me knows it's no secret that I love talking about superannuation and the power it has on your long-term financial security and retirement planning. Australia is one of the few countries in the world where you pay no tax in retirement. You can pay no tax on money in your pension account up to $2,000,000 from the 1 July 2025. Which is known as the Transfer Balance Cap (TBC).

Superannuation is often the quiet achiever when compared to other investments, as your hard-earned money is steadily building up to provide you with a comfortable retirement. But let's face it, it's easy to overlook because it's almost as if it's on autopilot, with contributions deducted from your pay cheque and deposited directly into your super fund.

Taking an active interest in your superannuation is essential. It's not just about knowing how much you've amassed over the years; it's about understanding where your money is being invested and how it's growing. Your risk profile can make a big difference. Having a conservative or a growth risk level could impact your retirement account significantly, and I have seen clients who would be $250,000 better offer if they opted for the right risk profile earlier on. The truth is, your superannuation is one of your most significant financial assets, possibly even exceeding the value of your home over time. Ignoring it is like ignoring a large treasure chest that's been gifted to you. This section looks at what superannuation is and the different ways it can be structured.

In Australia, it's mandatory for employers to make Superannuation Guarantee (SG) contributions to an employee-chosen super fund. But how do you decide which super fund best fits your needs? Currently this contribution is 12% of your gross income and is subject to changes in government regulations. This chapter aims to demystify the different types of superannuation funds, so you can make an informed decision that aligns with your goals and risk appetite.

But before you understand the various options in super funds it is important to understand some relevant terms.

Concessional contributions: These are pre-tax contributions, which include compulsory employer contributions and salary sacrifice contributions. They are taxed at a concessional rate, which is currently 15%. The maximum total amount of pre-tax contributions you can make in a year is currently $30,000, however, the government has made a great change and is allowing catch-up contributions over the last 5 years, subject to certain qualifying criteria. The main one is that you had a total superannuation balance (the total of all of your superannuation entitlements, wherever they may be in Australia) of less than $500,000 at the end of the prior financial year. This is a great way to boost superannuation and get a tax deduction. You can find out your catch-up amount on myGov or your tax agent can give you this information. In my opinion this is one of the best strategies to efficiently inflate your super that not many people know about. This strategy could also allow for one eligible spouse to make a catch-up contribution and transfer 85% of the contribution to their spouse under the spouse contribution splitting rules.

From the Australian Government:

> *A contribution split with your spouse is called a 'contributions-splitting super benefit' and is treated as a rollover to your spouse, not a new contribution for them. Accordingly, splitting your contributions with your spouse does not reduce the total contributions made for you or change their characteristics for the purposes of your contributions caps. For example, if you make a personal contribution and claim a tax deduction for it, that will count towards your concessional contributions cap for the year even if you then split and roll it over to your spouse. It will not count towards your spouse's cap.*[3]

As I have said, you don't know what you don't know, so it is important to investigate the options available to you under current legislation.

Non-concessional contributions: These contributions are made from after-tax income and are not subject to any additional tax when placed into super. The amount you can contribute currently is $120,000; however, you can pay 3 years at once (subject to meeting certain criteria), but you must be under the age of 75 (this is referred to as the "bring forward" rule). This law came into effect in 2022 and it amazes me that most people and new clients are unaware of the changes. This can make a massive difference if you receive an inheritance at 74. Hypothetically you would be able to put $360,000 into super then roll to a pension and never pay tax. See below chart. You can also do this for your spouse meaning you could get $720,000 into your super tax-free. This amount is indexed according to the prescribed formula annually. See table below from the ATO.[4]

Bring-forward cap first year (applying to 2024–25 and later years)

Total super balance on 30 June of previous year	Non-concessional contributions cap for the first year	Bring-forward period
Less than $1.66 million	$360,000	3 years
$1.66 million to less than $1.78 million	$240,000	2 years
$1.78 million to less than $1.9 million	$120,000	No bring-forward period, general non-concessional contributions cap applies
$1.9 million or more	nil	Not applicable

Contribution caps: There are limits to how much you can contribute to your super each year, both on a concessional and non-concessional basis. Exceeding these caps can incur additional tax.

Superannuation Guarantee (SG): This is the official term for compulsory superannuation contributions made by employers. It is currently set at 12% of an employee's ordinary time earnings. We recommend trying to pay additional super and increasing this rate to 15%, currently employers pay super quarterly, in the very near future employers will be required to pay this weekly. Over your lifetime this could possibly increase your super significantly.

Salary sacrifice arrangement: Salary sacrifice is an agreement with your employer to contribute a certain amount of your pre-tax salary or potential bonus into your super. The aim is to reduce your tax and boost your super balance at the same time. The word sacrifice doesn't really make this strategy sound appealing, but it has some great potential benefits.

- Salary sacrifice brings down your taxable income down.

- If you are a high-income earner, with combined income and concessional super contributions of more than $250,000, your concessional contributions above the $250,000 will be taxed at an additional rate of 15% (30% in total). However, this is still lower than the top marginal tax rate of 47% (including Medicare Levy).
- Salary-sacrificed super contributions are part of your concessional (or before-tax) contributions for the financial year. The concessional contributions cap includes mandatory contributions made by your employer and is $30,000 per year, regardless of your age.

The Government's MoneySmart website has a great super contributions optimiser calculator. It can give you an idea of how salary sacrificing can affect your super and take-home pay. If you like the idea of salary sacrificing, discuss it with your employer and see if you can make an arrangement with them. Most employers are open to such arrangements.

Preservation age: This is the minimum age at which you can access your superannuation benefits (currently from 1 July 2025 it is 60 for all), provided you have also retired. This is a common question and to put it simply, to access your super you must have triggered an event, for most this is retirement. However, this is different to the government age-pension qualification age, which is 67.

Transition to retirement (TTR): This is a strategy that allows individuals who have reached preservation age to access their super as a 'non-commutable' income stream while they're still working. It can be used to either reduce work hours or to boost super before full retirement. This can be used where a person wants to keep working but would love extra funds to pay off debt like their home loan or credit cards. For example, if you have $400,000 in super you can draw up to 10% each year to help with paying down debts or help you transition into retirement, and the payment can help with cutting your hours at work. I find a lot of my clients don't want to fully retire, so a TTR strategy can be beneficial. Paying off the home is the number one strategy I use with my clients, again it amazes me that no one knows about this; the government does a terrible job in educating the public. TTR payments from age 60 are tax free for the person receiving the TTR but the income is taxable on the earnings of the fund at 15% till age 65 then tax free.

Binding and non-binding death benefit nominations: This is a nomination made by a fund member to dictate who should receive their super benefits in the event of their death. We like to use non-lapsing binding nominations for our clients as once in place you don't have to go back every 3 years to renew, as is done by some industry super funds to ensure your nomination is still correct in the event of divorce or death. We work closely with lawyers that specialise in this area. A binding death benefit nomination is essentially the only mechanism through which you can dictate to the trustee of your fund how the death benefits must be paid (subject, of course, to the nomination being legally valid).

Risk adjusting: Think of 'risk-adjusting' like balancing on a seesaw. On one side, you've got the potential for high returns from your super investments, which sounds great, right? But on the other side, you have the risk of losing money if those investments don't perform well. Finding the perfect balance, so you're not too high or too low, is what risk adjustment is all about. For instance, you might be attracted to certain investments that promise high returns, such as private equity investment and some property trusts, but you must understand that higher returns come with higher risk. For example, a property trust might advertise 15% returns, however, they are also borrowing millions of dollars to do these developments. There are always risks surrounding delays in these developments, this can be due to council approval, finding trades people, builders or even delays in building materials. This was evident in relation to the Russian-Ukraine war as Australia sources most of our timber and building materials from Eastern Europe. If one of these events happens it can lead to lower returns and the possibility of losing all your money in certain circumstances.

On the other hand, you could go for a more diversified risk-adjusted portfolio, where the risk is spread between asset groups such as property, fixed interest, bonds, private equity, Australian shares and international shares, but the growth might be slower. That's where a financial adviser comes in handy. They'll help you understand your comfort level with risk and adjust your super investments accordingly. So, your super is working hard enough to grow your retirement savings but isn't likely to give you a nasty shock with big losses. The aim is to make sure your super is growing at a pace you're comfortable with, without causing you any sleepless nights worrying about taking on too much risk. At Virtual Financial our share portfolio only invests in companies with no debt billions in the bank and that pay dividends, We also reduce risk by investing in companies in various industries.

• • •

Remember, while understanding these terms is essential, individual circumstances vary significantly, and it's always wise to seek professional advice when making decisions about superannuation and other financial matters. Take the time to understand all these terms and discuss your appetite for risk with your spouse and financial adviser.

Now let's take a deep dive into the various options for investing your super funds.

Retail super funds (APRA regulated funds)

Retail super funds will often be one of your first encounters with superannuation. Typically they are managed by banks and investment companies and offer a convenient way of investing your money. Unlike a self-managed super fund (SMSF) they offer a range of pre-approved investment portfolios you can invest in.

One of the main attractions of retail super funds is their user-friendly platforms. With today's technology, you can monitor your superannuation at any time, from any place via handy phone apps or your home computer. It's a bit like having a live money tree in your backyard, where you can check on its growth every day! At Virtual Financial we use a Platform call Hub24 which is listed on the ASX and has over $100 billion on the platform.

Retail super, in most cases, has better insurance options that are fully underwritten providing you with the confidence that your insurance claim will be paid.

There are three types of insurance offered through your super, life cover, total and permanent disability (TPD) and income cover. I will explain these coverage options in the insurance section. The main reason you would pay for insurance under super is the tax benefit for life cover and TPD and cash flow for income cover. It's crucial to understand that some insurance policies have exclusions and are not underwritten until the time of claim. For instance, if you had a previous medical condition and you had a heart attack, the insurance company will try and get out of paying the claim. However, if you are fully underwritten, you may have paid a loading fee which means you pay more for your policy due to your existing medical condition (sometimes up to 200% more), but you may decide it's worth the extra cost to protect your family in a time of need.

Retail Super Funds, especially when complemented with sound financial advice, can serve as an excellent investment platform for those with less than $250,000 in superannuation. However a number of clients use the retail super with Hub24 and have in excess of $1 million. They combine a wide choice of investments with an easy-to-use platform, offering a good balance for many investors and is one that I will often recommend. Separately managed accounts (SMA) are used by our firm.

APRA regulated super funds: steady and secure

If we consider the structure of superannuation options as a pyramid, the APRA Regulated Superfunds form the sturdy base. These are your low-effort, trustworthy funds that offer a sense of security and simplicity.

Especially for balances below $250,000, APRA regulated super-funds can be one of the most cost-effective ways to start your super journey. The money is held in your name or through an APRA regulated superannuation fund. However, your control and transparency over the assets you're invested in can be less when compared to other options.

These funds offer a menu of investment options, allowing you to select and manage your investments according to your comfort and understanding. But do remember, while this arrangement does give you some control, there are certain factors to be aware of:

Trustee requirements: The trustee oversees these funds, meaning they set the rules about what investment strategies they'll accept and how much exposure an investor can have to these strategies. This may not always align with your personal investment goals.

SIS regulations: **liquidity:** The Superannuation Industry (Supervision) regulations ensure that your super fund can meet its financial obligations. These regulations require your fund to maintain a certain level of liquidity, limiting the fund's ability to invest in less liquid assets.

Corporate superannuation

When the mandatory Superannuation Guarantee started in 1992, corporate superannuation was created as a new ideal. All the big banks jumped at the opportunity to provide Superannuation to the big corporates. With this came automatic acceptance insurance, so staff with health conditions were able to get insurance they couldn't previously get access to. Fees were kept low but also the investment options were limited. To most Australians this didn't matter, as super was not on their radar and to some extent still isn't.

Unfortunately, the Australian Government removed all adviser fees from corporate super in 2019, and this led to all the corporate super funds sacking staff and ending the delivery of corporate super. We worked closely with AMP who had a great fund, but our business manager was retrenched and no one replaced him. Getting help is nearly impossible and so many corporate super clients are now left to work it out themselves. I hope that eventually the government implements a small fee to cover an adviser's time and effort for corporate super clients. Where corporate super can work really well is when you currently have a health condition, as there is no underwriting on corporate super. If your workplace has a corporate super option and you need insurance because perhaps your health isn't great, then I would recommend joining the fund and taking out what insurance you can.

We had an example of a client who was recovering from cancer and was in remission. The client took out corporate super and the insurances, including $800,000 life cover, were automatically included with no medicals. Twelve months later the cancer came back, but the client was able to provide life cover for her family. We used AMP as they had a great fund with attractive automatic insurances which include life, TPD and income cover.

Unfortunately, the days of corporate super for our firm are over as we cannot charge a fee, but corporate super should be an option if you really need the insurance. My advice would be to consult with an adviser to ensure you are set in the right investment options and cover all the other areas of financial advice including your will, retirement planning and investments.

For the majority of people, I believe retail super or SMSF's are much better options to create wealth and having the ability to risk-adjusted your portfolio, once the balance exceeds $250,000 for SMSF or below $250,000 for retail superannuation.

Industry superannuation

When it comes to planning for retirement, industry super funds often stand out as an attractive option. These funds are designed with members in mind, offering low fees and placing profits back into the fund to keep the costs down. However, I am wary of this model. I believe that super is not just about low fees but about providing advice and helping clients in a time of need. Industry super funds have their complexities and potential pitfalls.

The main issues with industry funds are as follows:

Transparency and control

Industry super funds can sometimes be a bit like a complex puzzle. Here are a few reasons why:

- **No control over investment selections:** Details like what the investment manager invests in, debt levels and covenants are often out of your reach.
- **Shared pooling system:** Accumulation and pension clients are often in the same pool. In a self-managed super fund (SMSF) all the benefits of franking credits, tax paid by companies, would go to the pensioner, giving the pension account credits. In an industry fund, it's like sharing a pie where not everyone gets an equal piece.

- **Estate planning uncertainty:** If you want more control and certainty around your estate planning, an SMSF often provides a superior outcome compared to APRA regulated funds.

Management concerns

These of some of the concerns I have regarding industry funds:

- **Integrity and skills of expertise:** Imagine having a board made up equally of employer-chosen and employee-chosen members. This can lead to challenges in decisions and governance.
- **Potential insider information:** Instances of senior executives benefiting from insider information have been observed.
- **Unannounced changes:** Your fund might change its investment parameters without notice, which is like changing the rules of a game mid-play.
- **Mismanagement costs:** If the fund is mismanaged, you will bear the cost. That's like being handed the bill for a dinner you didn't order!

Lack of flexibility and choice

- **No tailoring of solution:** Industry super funds often lack customisation. You might find yourself wearing a one-size-fits-all financial solution that doesn't fit your needs and goals.
- **Limited investment selections:** Your choices are restricted, akin to ordering from a limited menu.

Conflicts of interest and other concerns

- **Heavy union affiliation:** Some funds have strong ties to trade unions, which might influence investment decisions.
- **Advertising and investments:** Certain practices related to

advertising and investment funnelling through related entities might not align with your values and interests.

- **Group insurance challenges:** The terms of group insurance within these funds can change suddenly.

A cautionary tale

On so many occasions I've seen members be given no advice at all, and I've seen how detrimental that can be. I once had a new client approach me with a shocking story. Over the previous 10 years she saw no growth in her industry super fund. I thought it strange as the market had been doing well, and our client's funds had returned around 10% per annum on average. What surprised me is that they had invested her super in cash after the GFC and no one had advised her to change back. So, she missed all of those returns and she also had insurances coming out of the fund of around $8,000 each year, which explained why her superannuation guarantee payments by her employer were not increasing the balance of the fund. Luckily, she has 10 years of work left and we are helping her achieve her retirement goals by investing her funds into one of our risk-adjusted portfolios. We have managed to reduce the cost of her insurance by 60%. If she hadn't sought advice and stayed in an industry fund with low fees, she would have had a very tough retirement on the Centrelink pension.

Self-managed super funds (SMSF)

As we've explored the diverse landscape of superannuation, it's impossible to overlook the intriguing option of self-managed super funds (SMSFs). Imagine holding the steering wheel to your own financial journey, navigating through investments and making decisions tailored to your unique situation. SMSFs can provide control and customisation that some investors crave. However, this path isn't an easy option that can be set-up and forgotten about. There are complexities, legal responsibilities and intricate decisions that require careful consideration and expertise. It's an area so rich and multifaceted that we've dedicated an entire chapter to exploring the pros and cons of setting up an SMSF. We will take a deep dive into SMSFs, ensuring that you're well-equipped to understand if this might be the right path for your retirement journey.

Whether you opt for a retail super fund, corporate super, industry super or a SMSF, it's critical to seek advice and carefully evaluate the benefits and drawbacks. Ultimately, the choice should align with your financial goals and retirement aspirations.

Getting the right fund and the right investment mix is so important. As can be seen by following the case studies, ensuring you get this done is critical.

Too many people are enticed by low cost and low fees, but is this the answer? I believe the next 20 to 30 years will look very different to the last 20 to 30 years. The period of cheap interest rates seems to be over.

It is my opinion that interest rates will stay in a more normal position of 5–6% not the 2% that was on offer in the past. Asset classes will more than likely adjust and increase defensive assets, which are relatively low risk, such as government bonds and investment grade corporate bonds. A set-and-forget approach is not going to have the same level of returns that we have seen over the past 20 years.

It is my opinion if investment managers become too large, they are unable to access some great opportunities. Due to their size they are forced to invest in certain asset classes. Buying every share in an asset class is not how I invest when investing my clients in a retail fund. We use a manager to select 20 international and 20 Australian shares.

My philosophy is simple when using our MDA and involves establishing a portfolio with a strategic asset allocation, selecting high-quality, investment-grade securities and adopting a buy/hold approach as well as applying risk-adjusted returns and allowing changes to be make as needed. The MDA has uncorrelated investments such as Gold. When I talk about diversification, I'm not only talking about the asset classes but also the investment strategies.

Again, you don't know what you don't know, so it's best to trust the professionals when it comes to investing. I have so many clients that seek investment advice from their friends and family, which I do not advise.

ACTIVITY

Now is a great time to put this book down and look into the super fund you are currently using:

What fund are you using? Is it an industry fund, a retail fund, a corporate super plan or a SMSF?

Do you know and understand your appetite for risk?

Is your currently portfolio aligning with this risk profile?

Are the returns on investments meeting your retirement goals?

Is your fund risk-adjusted?

Beneficiary Nominations and Insurance within Super

In the previous chapter we looked at the various options available to you for investing your superannuation. In this chapter we will take a brief look at how you can ensure super funds are left to your requested beneficiaries and how to take advantage of insurance within your fund.

Firstly, let's start with a scenario. Imagine you've amassed a lovely super balance and suddenly something happens and you're not around anymore. Where does that money go? Enter beneficiary nominations. This allows you to instruct who your super will go to in the event of your death.

Beneficiary nominations

Types of Beneficiaries

Dependents: This could be your spouse, children or anyone financially reliant on you. The classes of dependent are defined in s 10 of the governing legislation: the Superannuation Industry (Supervision) Act 1993 (Cth).

Legal personal representative (LPR): Think of your LPR as the executor of your will.

Importantly, a superannuation death benefit must be a natural person, hence we refer to the legal personal representative rather than 'the estate'.

Binding vs non-binding nominations

Binding: This locks in your choice. Your super fund MUST pay your benefits to the nominated beneficiaries provided the nomination is valid.

Non-binding: This is more of a suggestion to your super fund. They'll consider your wish but also take into account other factors like relationship status.

> **TIP: Regularly update your nominations, especially after significant life events like marriage, divorce or having children.**

Insurance inside super

In the previous chapter we discussed having insurance within your superannuation, but what exactly does that mean? Many super funds offer insurance options as part of their package. This means you can be covered for certain events while your premium gets deducted from your super balance.

Types of Insurance

Life insurance (or death cover): Pays a benefit if you die or become terminally ill with fewer than 2 years to live.

Total and permanent disability (TPD) cover: If you're unable to work ever again due to serious injury or illness, this steps in.

Income protection: Think of this as a salary safety net. If illness or injury takes you out of work temporarily, this cover provides a percentage of your income. Can also provide a lump sum benefit in death.

Why consider it?

Convenience: Premiums are deducted from your super, so no direct out-of-pocket costs.

Affordability: Group buying often means cheaper rates.

Automatic acceptance: Many funds offer basic cover without health checks.

Why be wary?

Eroding your balance: Premiums can eat into your retirement savings.

Not always tailored: Generic policies might not cover your specific needs.

Caps and limits: There could be limits on claim amounts.

Tax is also an important consideration, particularly in circumstances in which significant levels of TPD cover is held. Income protection (or salary continuance as it is often referred to), if paid to the member by the trustee of the fund is not a superannuation benefit but ordinary assessable income and has tax applied as if you are receiving a salary.

TIP: Regularly review your insurance coverage. Ensure it fits your needs and isn't unduly eroding your super balance. It is also important to ensure that the life insurance is correctly structured with respect to ownership - this strategic objective could result in a more tax effective outcome in the event of a claim. For example, if the funds for life insurance are not going to a dependant but a friend or non-dependant sibling, then having the ownership outside of super makes sense as there will be no tax payable to the person receiving the life insurance.

Making your super work for you

Your super is more than just a retirement fund. It's a tool, a resource. With smart moves like setting up beneficiary nominations and understanding your insurance options, you can ensure it serves you (and your loved ones) well.

As always, don't hesitate to reach out for advice tailored to your unique situation. After all, our goal is a secure and stress-free retirement. Let's make it happen!

Self-Managed Super Funds

So, we've looked at the various options for investing your superannuation funds, delving into each category to understand their unique attributes, benefits and the potential drawbacks. What these options have in common is that once you have made an informed decision and monitor the outcome, especially at your yearly review with a financial adviser, there is not a lot that you need to do.

We're now going to explore self-managed super funds (SMSF) in more detail, which is one of the most personalised and potentially rewarding forms of investments. They are known for their flexibility and the greater degree of control that they offer you, the investor. We are going to look into their structure, the advantages, challenges and who this is suited to.

According to the Australia Tax Office (ATO):

> *Just under 612,000 SMSFs operate in Australia, with a combined membership of approximately 1.14 million Australians. The industry welcomed an additional 8,000 SMSFs over the September quarter of 2023 (latest available statistics) – the second largest period of growth in five years. But where has*

this demand come from? What is the profile of the average SMSF and its members? Approximately 93.1 per cent of SMSFs have less than three members. Approximately 77.6 per cent of members are over the age of 50, with just 3 per cent below the age of 35. NSW and Victoria dominate the SMSF industry, hosting over 62% of the national market. Just over 52% of members are male.[5]

Self-managed superannuation

This is money held in the name of the trustee of an SMSF on behalf of its members. The investor is able to invest in whatever assets they wish subject to the SIS legislation and the trust deeds or other restrictions placed on the investor. For example, there are limits placed on investing in assets, which are called in-house assets.

Starting out working at an accounting firm in Melbourne as a CPA and tax adviser, I found I was always talking in the past. I enjoy working more in the future and helping people get excited about having enough money for retirement, getting that investment property or investment portfolio. I believe SMSFs are a great way to invest your super, and it helps if you are as excited as I am about planning your financial future.

I've seen financial advice improving and becoming a lot more professional since I started. Because of my tax background as a qualified CPA and tax agent, I can give advice that my clients need all in one meeting. And that's important because you sometimes don't realise the tax implications with regards to your retirement investments. People who would like to have a property and investment portfolio need to know what the tax implications are and if you are working with an adviser who does not have that industry expertise you need to get your accountant involved with your decision making too. We will be covering tax in more detail later on.

Moving to a self-managed superannuation fund

Most people don't start out investing in a self-managed super fund (SMSF). The main reason for someone to move across to an SMSF is that they want more control of how their funds are invested, clients are sick of industry funds and retail funds that provide no advice and very few alternative investments that are not correlated to the share market, or a portfolio that is risk adjusted and very transparent. With a SMSF you are the trustee and it's up to you to ensure the investments are right and compliant. It starts with you, and that's what our clients love about SMSFs. And it is my hope that this chapter will encourage you to explore the options available to you.

Starting a SMSF can be an empowering step towards taking control of your retirement, but it's not for everyone. You need to be proactive and should typically invest in alternative assets that you wouldn't have access to in industry funds or other retail funds, such as commercial or residential property, direct shares and even crypto, Gold, private debt etc. By having that diversification of asset classes, you can diversify your funds and make informed decisions about where you invest. As an example, in an industry fund you can't invest in private equity or buy a residential property.

What exactly is a self-managed super fund?

When you have over $300,000 in super, a SMSF can be one of the best investment options you have. Essentially it is a trust fund with up to six members in the fund.

Generally speaking, it would be a couple, but it may also include siblings or children and can also include friends and business partners. Everyone's circumstance is different and I'm not going to tell you who you should include as that's something best discussed within your family and with your lawyers. Keep in mind that conflicts can arise, so clear agreements should be in place.

Establishing the fund

When setting up a self-managed super fund, there are a number of structures that need to be set up, we always recommend a company be used as the trustee and the members are then directors of the trustee company as it gives you the opportunity to invest in other assets (it also makes ongoing administration of the fund easier, particularly if you bring in more members and/or in the event of the death of a member). The trust deed is a legal document that outlines how the fund will be operated and needs to be carefully drafted with the help of a legal expert.

You will also need to register this with the ATO and obtain an Australian Business Number (ABN) and Tax File Number (TFN). You must also make sure the fund is compliant with all the relevant regulations. A bank account will also need to be set up in the name of the SMSF to manage the fund's operations.

Following this if you buy a property there's also a bare trust and another trustee company if the property is acquired through a borrowing mechanism referred to as a 'limited recourse borrowing arrangement'.

Costs involved and compliance

The estimated set-up could cost for a SMSF with a trustee company at Virtual Financial Advice will cost you $5,500 at time of writing. If you also bought a property, we would need to set up another Pty Ltd company and a bare trust to hold the property, which will cost an extra $1,100. This is required by the government to keep the property separate if there is debt. This includes a full financial planning meeting with an adviser. You should also be aware of the ongoing costs, which include management fees, auditing costs and other administrative expenses. We normally see these costs at around $2,500 to $3,500 per year.

I believe once you have over $400,000 to setup your SMSF, the ongoing costs are manageable, especially when compared to an industry fund. We do a full cost-analysis in our financial plan comparing the fees of your previous fund to the new fees you will pay.

One very important point is that a full financial plan must be done before any structures are set up. It surprises me that accountants are still setting up these structures with no advice. If you want to stay off the ATO's radar I would recommend seeing a qualified financial adviser. It is really important to get the right advice to ensure everything stacks up. We have taken over a number of SMSF property funds from other advisers where the client was frustrated by a lack of cash flow owing to the absence of a 5-year plan. Getting the right advice is essential before buying a property.

We often find that clients and other advisers have not done this and have neglected to take into account insurance expenses, tax and filing expenses and expenses on the property such as repairs agent commissions etc. They then find themselves having to put more funds in the market to make it work.

It is important that you follow the legal requirements and file a set of accounts and a tax return with the ATO every year. On average this will cost around $2,500 depending on what is in the fund each year, plus the fee for your adviser. The adviser service fee is for advice during the year and may include a retirement plan, contribution strategy, insurance recommendations etc. At Virtual Financial Advice we charge a flat fee of $165 per month and 0.66% of the funds invested. You start to really get the benefits from a cost point of view once you have a solid base of funds in your self-managed super fund, and obviously as that increases, your benefits will be greater as well.

It is important to note that having over $400,000 in super is where you really start to see significant changes in costs. You want to ideally have at least $300,000 in your super fund before you switch into a self-managed super fund.

Develop an investment strategy

It is important that the trust fund members have a clear understanding of their goals and risk appetite. Take the time to determine what assets you will invest in, how will you balance risk and return, and what are your needs in terms of access to liquid funds?

Plan how you are going to reach these goals. For example, are you going to invest in an MDA, or buy a property? What rent are you going to receive? Is there a shortfall? Have you got enough cash flow? Can you fund this or is there a need to borrow funds?

As you are the trustee and in charge of what happens to your fund and where to invest, unlike an industry fund, you are not investing with the masses and have an opportunity to get creative and be different. You are one that makes the decisions about where and how to invest. We use managed discretionary accounts (MDA) for our clients, but some clients then may go and invest in private equity, Gold, investment properties, crypto etc. The investment options are numerous and at Virtual Financial Advice we have a number of approved investments for our clients that go through a strict investment process. We look at these options in more detail later on. It is my belief that you need to have a risk adjusted portfolio that is not just aligned to the stock market or property.

Having a SMSF can be the safest way to invest, as the investments are in the name of the SMSF and not in the name of a superannuation trustee such as in an industry fund where you have no decision-making power. An example of this was when the husband of one of my clients died and had an industry fund and a SMSF. She first tried to get funds from the industry fund to help pay for the funeral, and was very upset when she was advised it was a long process with a number of forms that needed approval by their trustee. I advised her that she is the trustee with the SMSF and could ask for $30,000 as a death benefit to pay for her husband's funeral. Flexibility is one of the major benefits of a SMSF.

Top 3 investments for Australians

Property

The most popular investment is property. It is the biggest asset class in the world and there is a cultural mindset related to the safety of property investment due to its tangibility. It also allows for increased options for borrowing to invest within a self-managed super fund. This is not about purchasing a home to live in, it's a property you will collect rent on and manage as an investment.

Property is a great way to invest. I've been in the game now for over 30 years and in that time, property has done very well. I'm a big fan of property, but like everything it's only going to go up if you buy the right property, so we recommend you use a buyer's agent. As a financial adviser I don't give property advice, but we do the financial analysis for our clients using the latest software. It's amazing the detail they go into to ensure the property suits your individual needs. They look at location, the street, what type of neighbours there are, growth potential etc.

If you're not an expert, but you really want to buy an investment property, working with a buyer's agent is your best option, and the expense will be paid by the SMSF. What you should look at when researching investment properties is what the additional costs will be and what the projected returns will be in 5, 10, 20 and 30 years. This forecasting will help give an indication of whether buying property will be a worthwhile investment. This is where your financial adviser can help you determine the returns and risk analysis.

Managed discretionary accounts (MDA)

The second biggest investment we have is our managed discretionary account (MDA), we love the versatility it gives and later on we will look at these in more detail. Essentially you can use an MDA to really help you invest. It's important to take the time to investigate the portfolio you invest in and ensure it matches your appetite for risk. I use the platform Hub24 for managing our client MDA portfolios and use a dealer group as the investment manager.

This allows you to manage your discretionary account, while your adviser can oversee the portfolio for you and make required changes at any time. If, for example, the market goes down or you need to change the cash or move to fixed interest you can make these changes at any time. This means that a SMSF gives you the opportunity to have your funds invested in the best way possible to meet your retirement goals, in a risk adjusted portfolio.

As discussed in the previous chapter some industry funds have done quite well, but I think the issues lie in the lack of diversification and uncorrelated assets as well as not getting the advice that potentially hurts members' overall return on investment. And that's the benefit of an SMSF and an MDA: you are in control.

When the markets start going down, funds have easily dropped 10–20%. I've seen this happen when an industry super fund has dropped 20% and there's no news about it, therefore most investors have no idea they have lost money. These funds also only have to value their assets every three to five years. Whereas when you are using an MDA, assets are valued daily, so your knowledge and preparation for change is current at all times.

Shares

The third most popular option is shares. Some people have a strong interest in the share market and may set aside a certain portion of their fund, normally around 10–20% to invest themselves. We have seen clients use Commsec and I have also recommended the Chartist that helps investors with education and investing in shares. When we use shares, we would normally go with direct shares and use an SMA to hold them. We are currently using private portfolio managers (PPM) to hold our portfolios. The portfolios only contain around 20 stocks in either an international fund or an Australian fund. The shares we own in most cases have no debt, billions in the bank and pay dividends each year to the shareholders. Most are household names such as Amazon and Microsoft.

The pros and cons

When talking to clients about moving into a SMSF it can be overwhelming, and I find this list can help with understanding the ins and outs of what's involved.

Pros:

- Effective tax management as SMSF benefit from concessional tax rates and the timing of when tax is paid
- Reduced costs of running fund once you have a certain amount of money in your fund
- Protection from creditors as super does not form part of bankruptcy
- Control of how and where you invest your funds that can also include gearing in property and shares
- Access to investments not available in retail or industry funds ie. crypto, Chartist, Blue Oceans, Private Equity etc. Being able to invest in uncorrelated assets such as unlisted property and Gold, private debt funds, infrastructure investments
- Invest in collectables such as artwork
- Estate planning i.e. have your kids join the fund and transfer your wealth easily
- Pay for life, TPD and income insurance cover through your SMSF
- The ability to purchase an investment property in your SMSF
- The ability to set up an MDA

Cons:

- You must keep records and do accounts, tax return and an audit each year
- Costs of running the fund, when it is a lower balance
- Need at least $250,000 to make it cost effective
- Fines for non-compliance can be high
- The temptation of investing yourself and taking on too much risk
- It takes time and effort to keep up to date with your SMSF; it's not a flick and forget strategy
- You need to spend money on the set up, which may involve trustee companies and bare trusts
- Government changes to SMSF law including borrowing changes, which would affect the purchase of a property
- SMSF members must be Australian citizens or permanent residents
- Restrictions on dispute resolutions in the event trustees are unable to obtain legal assistance. Retail funds can get help from APRA and ASIC

Self-managed super funds offer an attractive way to have greater control over your retirement funds and potentially achieve better returns through diversification and investment in non-traditional assets. However, it requires significant responsibility, financial knowledge, time commitment and the willingness to adhere to legal compliance. This is why it's important to work with a team of professionals including your financial adviser, accountant, lawyer, buyer's agent and the members of the SMSF.

If you're considering an SMSF, take the time to understand your own financial situation, investment goals, risk tolerance and whether you have the capability and interest in managing your own fund. Consider the benefits of working with financial professionals who can guide you through the process and help you make informed decisions. The ATO have a number of helpful articles to read and consider.

Remember, the choice to move into a self-managed super fund is a significant one and should be made with careful consideration and professional advice. By being proactive, informed and with the support of the right professionals, you can create a successful self-managed super fund that aligns with your retirement aspirations and gives you the flexibility to have your money working for you.

PART THREE

Investment Philosophy

At Virtual Financial we have 2 main philosophies to investing our clients' funds.

Strategy 1

Is to invest our clients into a share portfolio where we only select 20 stocks in the global fund and 20 stocks in the Australian Fund. Depending on their risk profile we also can include cash fixed interest bonds.

The performance of the portfolio has been nothing short of first class with the Global Fund returning 34% last year as at 31 August 2025 and averaging 25% over the last 5 years.[6]

The fund overall last year averaged 23 % considerably higher than industry funds with low fees. As I explain to my clients its not just about fees but returns. As we are a boutique fund we are able to invest in smaller portfolio's the big industry funds have to invest in hundreds of funds as they are investing billions.

We use the number one platform Hub24 for our clients and then invest using Separately Managed Accounts (SMA) and investments such as PPM.[7]

Strategy 2

We use MDA for our clients where the total funds exceed $300,000 and that want more diversification I have explained the MDA below but in summary its to help client's that want assets that are not correlated with the share market, that will react differently if the share market falls. It's to give clients more comfort during times when markets are volatile. Returns of the MDA are specific to the person who invests as not every MDA is the same. We build the MDA to suit the client and their risk profile and wishes.

Rule of 72

I always explain to my clients the power of compound interest and returns. I had a client with an industry fund returning 4% per annum over the last 5 years and our fund had returned 12% per annum over 5 years.

The rule of 72 shows you how many years it takes to double your money dividing 72 into your return. So, a 4% return would take 18 years to double your money where a 12% return would only take 6 years. The power of compound returns is amazing and should be a focus, instead of focussing on fees. As a result, a lot of people miss the opportunity.

That is when getting the right advice can make a big difference.

Managed Discretionary Accounts

Throughout this book we have mentioned managed discretionary accounts (MDA) but what exactly are they? I think of them as your investment superheroes, and this chapter looks at demystifying another tool that will help you reach your financial goals.

Understanding managed discretionary accounts

MDAs are like the Swiss-army knife of investment management. They offer an array of benefits and keep things flexible and efficient. But let's break it down into bite-sized pieces.

In simple terms, an MDA is an investment service where a custodian (think of them as a financial guardian) holds assets on your behalf. An investment manager takes the reins, making buy-and-sell decisions to grow your money.

How they are structured

MDAs can be built within three main structures:

- **Ordinary money:** Regular investments outside superannuation
- **SMSF (self-managed super fund):** Investments within your very own super fund
- **APRA regulated fund:** Investments within a regulated fund platform

Proactive management: the MDA superpower

The benefit of investing with an MDA is they take investment management to the next level, offering:

- **Instant reactions:** Unlike traditional processes, where decisions might be made once or twice a year, MDAs allow instant changes. Quick decisions can save significant benefits. During COVID, as an example, the ability to act quickly to avoid significant downturn in the market.
- **Equality among clients:** With MDAs, whether you're a big fish or a small fry, changes to portfolios with the same risk profile are made simultaneously.
- **Wholesale rates and techniques:** Investment managers transact using savvy broking techniques, all at wholesale rates.
- **Legal ownership and benefits:** It's yours, and yours only.

Having legal ownership of the investments in your portfolio means:

- **Keeping what's yours:** All the income and capital gains are retained.

- **Tax perks:** Benefits like franking credits are yours, and you'll be insulated from the ups and downs of other investors
- **Scale and efficiency:** Big benefits for your wallet
- **Consolidated reporting:** Everything in one place, keeping things simple
- **Bulk ordering:** This lowers costs, meaning more savings passed on to you

MDAs in action: your 24/7 investment watchdogs

The power of MDAs lies in their constant vigilance and flexibility. We, as financial planners, can:

- **Make changes anytime:** If the market stumbles or opportunities arise, adjustments can be made instantly.
- **Personalised strategy:** Your portfolio is tailored according to your needs, and a professional oversees it, making sure it stays on track.

Making MDAs work for you

MDAs are all about putting you in control of your investment but also gives you a professional to guide the way. From the safety of the SMSF structure to constant monitoring and the ability to act instantly, MDAs offer a robust and flexible approach to investing.

Feel like this might be the right path for you? Or still scratching your head? That's what financial advisers are here for. An MDA gives you an advantage for risk-adjusted returns as you can invest in uncorrelated assets including Gold, private debt, unlisted property including NDIS property, infrastructure, fixed interest. We have clients that invest in real Gold not just Gold listed on the ASX. They can go to the Australian Mint and can see their Gold.

Navigating Alternative Assets: A Balanced Approach to Growing Your Money

What are alternative assets?

Alternative assets are the added bonus to your investment strategy. They add diversity and can be what keeps you excited about your portfolio. They include investment properties, cryptocurrencies (like Bitcoin) or a business. These options aren't your run-of-the-mill stocks or bonds, but they can be a fantastic way to spice up your investment strategy.

Crypto: the digital gold rush

While many see cryptocurrencies as the future of money, it's essential to approach with caution and knowledge.

Thrill and risk: Imagine putting all your money into crypto and then watching your portfolio drop by 50% overnight. Yes, it can happen, and it's not a good feeling.

Balanced approach: Here's my golden rule – no more than 10–20% of your investments in crypto. It's all about moderation and diversification. This is the alternative investment space.

The importance of professional guidance: By working with an adviser, you take emotions out of the equation. We look at facts, not feelings, to ensure your money is invested wisely, based on a well-thought-out strategy.

Investment properties: building wealth, brick by brick

Real estate has always been a popular investment avenue and here's why:

Long-term growth potential: Property values tend to grow over time, providing a reliable investment path.

Rental income: Owning a rental property can provide a steady stream of income.

Considerations and risks: It's not all rosy; there are costs such as maintenance, taxes and potential market downturns. Working with a buyer's agent who understands the market conditions can help elevate some of these risks and take away the associated emotion.

Everything You Should Know When Buying an Investment Property

This chapter is written in collaboration with buyer's agent Colin Lee as I do not give property advice but understand property is a significant asset and my clients love property.

Why use a buyer's agent?

I have seen clients who have used project marketers and other agents who really don't act in the best interest of clients. We don't want our clients to go through that. We want them to see a buyer's agent or someone reputable in the market. Financial advisers must act in the best interest of the client and not prioritise commissions or fees. The same should apply to other professionals assisting you in your journey to financial freedom.

There are two different types of buyer's agents. Ones that get paid by the developer or builder are more commonly known as project marketers. The misconception for most people is that they think that all agents representing a seller are buyer's agents.

I've seen some seller's agents that would call themselves buyer's agents so you have to be mindful of which party the agent is actually representing. Legally speaking, the client is the party that pays the fee for a service. In financial services, if I pay you a fee for a service, I am your client, and you are responsible for my financial wellbeing. And that financial adviser will not be motivated by commissions. The fees are the same regardless of what financial products or platforms are used.

Project marketers, or what we call sales agents, that purport themselves to be buyer's agents are actually accountable to the sellers themselves. Whether that's the actual seller of the property or the developer or the builder. Those parties pay them a marketing fee, or commission to sell a particular property. Now it may not be a known fact, but real estate agents charge anywhere between 2–3% for the fee that they would charge to a seller should they be successful in a sale of a particular property.

Similar to a project marketer who gets paid anywhere from 3–6%. So that's how they get paid and are therefore not really responsible for your wellbeing because their vested interest is in getting the highest possible price for the developers.

Some buyer's agents would charge a percentage and some buyer's agents would charge a fixed fee. So, if you were to engage a buyer's agent, be mindful of the fee structure. Colin from Inspire Realty charges a fixed fee for service, but every agent is different. I believe that if you're building an investment property portfolio and engaging the services of a buyer's agent, there shouldn't be a difference in the quality of this service whether you're buying a $700,000 property or a $1,000,000 property. In most cases, exactly the same effort goes into finding any of those properties. So that's the reason why I prefer fixed fee, because then they're not necessarily motivated by the actual purchase price of a property.

As an example, if Colin can find you an $800,000 property that's worth $850,000 and thus saving you $50,000, it's certainly a much better deal than you buying from the sellers' agent as there is no incentive to sell it at a lower price. When a buyer's agent charges you a fixed fee, the motivation is to find the right investment property at the right price, without ulterior motive.

I have certainly heard some horror stories from clients. As an example, a client had an SMSF and was talked into buying property in a retirement village worth $320,000. There was no growth over an 8-year period, which was going to affect their retirement. This could have been avoided with the right professional advice from someone not influenced by commissions or the seller. Hence why I believe a buyer's agent is necessary.

Insights from a buyer's Agent with Colin Lee

There are many different types of properties, and one of the things that we focus on as a buyer's agent is purchasing properties in established suburbs with a larger block of land. One of the things I like to show my clients is the fact that land appreciates and buildings depreciates. You must therefore be very careful about purchasing units. I'm sure there are buyer's agents out there that will believe in investing in units but, I don't believe there is a lot of opportunity for you to make money on a unit. At the end of the day, the building has a number of units in that development that you're competing against at the time of sale, so it's very hard to make genuine money on a unit. You must have a point of difference if you are buying a unit, such as good views or be placed in an attractive area.

There are many different types of buyer's agents. Some that would focus on units, townhouses and house and land. For us, we focus on properties that have a land component because you can manufacture value on those properties. The truth is that there's only so much you can do to improve the value of a unit. And we know that the way to make money is to buy something that you can either land-bank for future development or you can manufacture value in that property by spending a little bit of money. I've assisted clients where they've bought a block of land with a property and they've subdivided it, and they've sold one of them off and kept the main property. They have then built a second property and made money from that sale.

Another example is if it's a 3-bedroom, 1 bathroom property, you can add a fourth bedroom or a second bathroom and that's how you manufacture value on that property. So, it's about manufacturing value and that's why a lot of the properties that we procure for our clients end up making a lot of money, because you can see the potential of the property. It's not just purchasing a property.

In the US, you must have a buyer's agent to represent you to negotiate with the sellers' agent. You can't just go knock on a door with the seller's agent and say I want to purchase this property. Maybe there are some pockets that would still do that, but certainly for the higher end properties, you'd normally have a buyer's agent that represent you as a client. One of the key reasons why people would use a buyer's agent is because what you don't know, you don't know, and that can be very dangerous. I think too many people don't have the right reason for buying a property.

How to know what to invest in?

There's actually an art and a science to building an investment property portfolio. Let me just focus very quickly on the science. Over the years, I've learned that the most sophisticated and the best professional property investors purchase properties as if they're running a business.

There are certain key criteria that we consider as a buyer's agent. We prefer to purchase in areas with higher owner-occupancy rates. Suburbs with higher owner occupier ratios will have stronger demands for those properties in the future. Owner-occupiers would pay any emotional price versus an investor. You will most likely attract owner-occupiers at the time of selling a property in your property portfolio.

We also look at vacancy rates. 9 out of 10 people that buy investment property don't look at this metric. Vacancy rate will show the rentability of that particular suburb, and you want it to be as low as possible. The lower the vacancy rate, the higher the demand for that property.

Then there are things like long-term growth rates, percentage rental growth rate. These are all numbers that we look at as professional investors that a normal person would not even consider. What most people don't realise is that just because the numbers check out doesn't mean that's a good property. We know there are good streets and they are bad streets within a suburb, right? So that's where the art of searching for property comes into hand.

We have found a lot of people are too busy. They work full-time and need to prioritise their families. And so, they neither have the capacity, nor the interest, nor the energy to go around on the weekends to go look at property. Something I learned from my property mentor is that you need to have seen, at the very minimum, 50 properties before you make one offer. Too many people just get too tired. They go for two inspections on the weekend; they see 10 properties and they make an offer. Well, I don't think seeing 10 is a bigger enough pool.

It's like going out and meeting 10 girls in your entire life and then marrying one of them. You have to actually get familiar with the suburb, with the type of properties. The reason for this is to avoid overpaying. Unless you've got the time to go and see 50 at the very least, you're not making an informed and a sensible decision.

It is important to look at the cash flow and rental yield across the last 10 years. Look at the capital growth, because history tends to repeat itself. If you know the capital growth rates of the last five years, it's probably a pretty good indication of the capital growth rates of the next five years.

There are some aspects we consider non-negotiables when considering an investment property. Firstly, flood zones must be avoided when you're looking at an investment property. It's amazing how many people buy investment properties in flood affected areas. There are apps to help with this. Some clients buy well priced properties thinking they've found a bargain and haven't considered that Brisbane floods regularly and much of the city is in a flood zone. The resale value is affected and insurance premiums will be high; both will affect your return on investment.

Secondly, bush fire zones. There are degrees to bush fire zones; we would never recommend properties in heavily effected zones due to the danger. Many areas are prone to bushfires, but you don't want to invest in areas that have been historically affected.

You should also avoid places that have easements as this could affect the viability of the property. If you have a sewer line running through the property, this will impact development in the future. Same goes for powerlines or nearby roads, particularly highways. Heritage listing is also important to consider as it will affect your ability to develop or renovate the property.

The reason why a lot of my clients appreciate our service or the service of a buyer's agent in general, is because we know the area. It's one thing to tick the box in terms of the numbers and it's another to consider the demography of the neighbourhood and the likelihood that your property will be affected by severe weather or impeded in development. Your buyer's agent can help do this work for you to ensure you're as informed as possible before you buy.

I have a client that spent 6 months looking for a property and made 5 offers. None of them were successful because she doesn't know how to deal with the agents. She's just trying to get a good deal, but making an offer that is way off will ensure that you are unsuccessful. There is an art to putting forward an offer; it's not always just about the price.

Sometimes it's about being able to negotiate with what the sellers want. We had a situation where the seller wanted to live in the property for another 3 months before settlement because they hadn't found a place to move to. So, negotiations also involved an extended settlement. By finding out what the sellers want, you can use this in negotiations, which you can only do if you have a good relationship with the agent. We can facilitate the best terms to negotiate the best deals.

In today's market, what we're finding is that it takes 5 offers before one is accepted. Once the third or fourth offer is rejected, people get desperate and start offering much more extortionate figures. If you've already overpaid and are paying more, you've lost. I've learnt that you make money on a property at purchase, not when selling time comes around.

Many people make emotional decisions when they purchase property because they get overwhelmed by the whole process and want it over with at any cost. This can lead to making ill-informed decisions that aren't research and data driven. It's an emotional decision that they've made because they have been told that they're close. We can take the emotion out of the process.

Structure for investment property

A common question overlooked by investors is the structure. Most investors put the property in both spouses' names. But if one spouse is earning $250,000 and the other is earning $50,000, we would want the loss on a negatively geared property to be offset against the higher-earner entirely.

I have had clients come and see me and say that they bought an investment property in their trust as they thought this would be safe but didn't realise that losses are stuck in the trust and can only be offset by income in the trust. You can certainly use trusts and companies, but you would have to get the right advice on when to use them.

I would normally recommend a trust if they have a high-risk job where they could be sued, such a surgeon. Protecting assets is very important and should be of consideration when purchasing an investment property. There are many paths to building wealth. I'd probably say the best course of action is engaging a financial planner and consulting your accountant to decide which is the best entity or platform.

When you purchase a property and decide to change the entity because you have made a mistake, you have to pay stamp duty. When you change any names on a title of a property or change names on the entity the contract is in, it can be costly. I made that mistake when I started out my journey as I just wanted the tax-deductible expense, so I'd just buy properties under my own name without knowing the risks involved with purchasing property under my individual entity.

Real estate agents and financial advisers are at risk of being sued, so the tax deduction in this case may not be the key reason for deciding what entity to put this in. Everyone has got different needs and different risk profiles.

I've seen people make offers on property only to sign a contract under their own entity when they're actually purchasing it under SMSF or under a trust. Just make sure you get good advice, because once you authorise and you sign the contract, you are locked in, and it may cost you stamp duty to change the structure.

Get good advice

There's no going back on the entity of the contract. There are 5 main entities we use:

- Individual names
- Partnership or joint names
- Trust structure with trustee company
- Company
- SMSF

Having the right advice in this area is critical for your success in investing in investment properties. Have the right team of accountants, financial advisers, loan brokers and buyer's agents is critical in getting this right.

In my 25 years in this industry, I've seen many developments Unfortunately, property is not regulated by ASIC and there are lot of agents selling properties for commissions only and not acting in the best interest of their clients. In my experience, clients do best when engaging a buyer's agent, buying house and land and doing their own homework.

Getting the numbers done is very important and at Virtual Financial Advice we invest heavily in the best software to benefit our clients.

PART FOUR

Insurance Planning

What Do You Have That's Worth Protecting?

Life is filled with unexpected twists and turns, and having the right insurance policies in place is like carrying an umbrella; it might not prevent the storm, but it will provide protection when it hits.

At Virtual Financial Advice we always say that the ultimate aim of insurance is to give you peace of mind. When Ant and Emily got together, each had children from previous marriages. Emily was divorced and her three sons and daughter were very young. So, she had to care for her children full-time. Ant was divorced, had his children on weekends and paid child support for them to his ex-wife. He had also settled the financial specifics of his divorce before meeting Emily.

The insurance that Ant and Emily require is quite different. Ant needs life cover not only to pay out personal debts but also the business debt, as no debt should be left in the event of death. Yes, you can sell properties and a business but at that time you want to have choice. Having insurance that will pay out all the debt gives Emily peace of mind. It will also help leaving his 3 kids money for their future, something he always wanted.

Ant may also consider TPD in case he is totally and permanently disabled and can no longer work. A lump sum can be used to pay down debts and help with medical expenses and alterations to the home if necessary.

Ant could also consider trauma insurance. This covers around 60 conditions including heart attack, stroke and cancer. We normally recommend enough to cover loan repayments for 2 years and an amount for medical costs, normally around $150,000. The last insurance Ant should consider is income cover, to help cover his wages in a time of sickness or accident.

We would recommend Emily consider life, TPD and trauma cover, but as she does not have a business, her levels of cover will be different. We use a detailed spreadsheet to calculate exactly what our clients need; from this we work with the clients to see what they want and can afford. Insurance companies will not cover you in certain circumstances or will put loadings on to the policy, which increases the cost of the premium. Exclusions may also be added meaning that if you have an existing condition or injury, you will not be covered for issues relating to that condition or injury.

When it came time to marry and buy a house to live in, Emily and Ant wanted it to be a jointly owned property. But putting all their respective resources into one property was just too complex for their respective situations. Instead, they kept their finances separate and paid a deposit to purchase their property together, because they had both been divorced before, had separate investment properties and Ant had a successful business worth around $500,000.

Now, years later, they have options, grandchildren, a joint family home, some separate investments and family dynamics to also consider. When Emily's mother passed away in England there were additional complications concerning her children's inheritance.

Working with a financial planner is about more than just deciding on which kind of investments and superannuation is most suitable, because everyone's situation is different. What do you have now that needs protection? What is the insurance process? The following 8-step process is what we use to help our clients determine what insurance policies are right for them and will help navigate those unexpected life events.

Step 1: Understanding the types of insurance you need

Life cover: Offers a lump-sum benefit for your loved ones in case you pass away or are diagnosed with a terminal illness with less than 2 years to live.

Total and permanent disability (TPD): This provides a lump sum payment if you suffer a permanent disability that prevents you from working or performing daily life activities.

Trauma insurance: This pays out a lump sum if you're diagnosed with a severe illness like cancer or have a heart attack or a stroke (at least 68% of trauma claims).[8] It's meant to help with medical costs and everyday expenses during a tough time. As a guide our clients use it to pay 2 years of home loan repayments and $50,000 for medical expenses.

Income cover: If you're unable to work due to illness or injury, this insurance provides a replacement income to help with daily living costs. 1 in 3 Australians will be off work for more than 3 months before turning 65 due to sickness or injury. More than half of all serious accidents happen outside of work, so workers' compensation doesn't always apply.[9]

Step 2: Calculate the amount required

The next step is to calculate how much insurance you'll need. Remember, this amount should cover any debts, ongoing expenses and provide a safety net for your loved ones. At virtual financial we use a detailed questionnaire that calculates how much you need. We consider the following:

- Funds required for funeral expenses
- Pay off home loan
- Pay off investment property loans
- Private schooling
- Lump sum for a spouse to stay home and look after children
- Medical expenses
- Income replacement

Step 3: Identify assets to reduce insurance costs

Some assets, like an investment property, could be used to offset the cost of life insurance. We don't recommend this option as we believe you should have a choice, and you don't want to have to hastily sell properties. But if the cost of insurance is high then this is an option. For example, if you have a $500,000 investment property loan you may choose not to insure that and incur the cost as you could possibly sell the asset and clear this debt.

Step 4: Identify debts to pay out or retain

It's essential to have a plan to handle your debts in case of any unexpected life events. Which ones do you want to pay out and which ones do you want to retain? We would normally recommend paying out all debts if something happens to you as you want to have choices in what you do. Income cover will also be paid in most cases, and this could also help in the event of sickness or an accident.

Step 5: Determine the gap

Here, we compare with what you have to what you need. This step will highlight any gaps in your coverage that need to be addressed. We will then discuss and determine how much you can afford and how this may impact your retirement plan.

Step 6: Value for money

Remember, not all insurance policies are created equal. It's important to compare products to find the best value for your money. We work with a number of companies and our software analyses the costs and features of all the insurance products. There have been some new entrants to the Australian market like Metlife and Neos, which have been really sharp in pricing. We are also platinum partners with some insurance providers giving our clients extra discounts up to 27%.

Step 7: The application process

When working with Virtual Financial Advice there is no need to worry, we take care of this for you. If you are doing it on your own, I recommend reading the fine print, answering all questions honestly and providing all requested paperwork.

Step 8: Understanding the claims process

This can be the most daunting step for people. In the event you have to make a claim it will no doubt be a stressful time. It will make things easier if you understand the claims process and if possible, have someone work with you. At Virtual Financial Advice we take care of the claims process for our clients. We work closely with insurance providers and understand the level of detail they require when making a claim. We have seen insurance companies deny claims due to insufficient paperwork. We have taken over a number of these claims and have had the claims paid out in full. It is interesting to know which companies are difficult at claim time and it's our job to ensure we are working with the best companies that are going to perform when its needed. If we do have any trouble we will fight the claim for you at no charge.

According to the Royal Commission into Misconduct in the Banking, Superannuation and Financial Services Industry, insurance companies are losing several billion dollars a year just in paying out income protection claims in Australia. So, it's not that people are not getting paid. Insurance companies do pay out and, in most cases, we haven't had a problem for our clients.

In Ant and Emily's case, their financial case is complex, with several factors to consider: multiple properties, a business, inheritances and a blended family. The crucial areas we would recommend they, and all clients, consider insuring include:

Income: A loss of income, particularly for the primary earner, Ant, could have severe impacts on their lifestyle. Income protection insurance is essential for peace of mind.

Assets: Their home, business and other properties need to be protected. This could be through home insurance, landlord insurance for investment properties and business insurance.

Inheritance: If an inheritance is expected, there could be implications for their overall financial plan. Life insurance could help protect the value of this.

Debt: Life insurance can ensure that any outstanding debts are paid off upon the death of a family member, preventing a financial burden on surviving family members.

Everyone's situation is unique, so it's important to have open discussions about your financial situation with your financial planner. They can help you navigate through these complex decisions and ensure you and your loved ones are protected.

Real life examples: How Virtual Financial Advice would advise our clients

Kieran and Caitlin: We would start by looking at income protection, TPD, life and trauma insurance. At this stage of their life the cover does not have to be too high as they have no debt. But as they are looking at buying a property, it would be ideal to get the insurance in place before they purchase their home and are still young and healthy enough to avoid high premiums or exclusions.

Nic and Talisha are in their thirties, have a child and lots of life ahead of them. It is important to look at ensuring they are financially secure if the worst-case scenario happens. We would look at covering them for life and TPD, trauma insurance and income cover, as they have debt. Life and TPD will help pay that off and they may wish to have funds to send their children to private schools, Trauma insurance will help with a one-off payment to pay for the mortgage and medical costs, and income cover will ensure the income keeps coming in. As I tell all my clients, the only way their retirement goals will be met is if they have income. 11% of bankruptcies are from people getting sick and having no income to pay the mortgage.

Joe and Mark are on good incomes and have no plans for children. We would look at life cover and TPD to pay out debts cover medical expenses, trauma cover to cover 2 years of mortgage repayments and an amount for medical expenses, and income cover with a 6-month wait, as they have enough reserve cashflow, and a 5-year benefit period. Research by AIA have confirmed 90% of cases for income cover are settled within 2 years.

Karen on the other hand, has no commitments and no dependents. Therefore, she would not require life insurance, however, she would need TPD and trauma insurance to cover home loan repayments and immediate medical expenses. Income cover is very important for Karen, and she would look at a 30-day wait, as she does not have a lot of reserve money, and benefit until age 65.

Ant and Emily have a complex situation and given Ant's properties, business and their family situation, an insurance policy of around $3.5 million might be advisable. This would cover his debts, provide for Emily and leave an inheritance for their children. It might seem a hefty sum, but it's a protective shield for his family against life's uncertainties. At their age they will have to weigh up the cost benefit of TPD insurance and trauma insurance. Income cover is advisable for Ant with a 90-day wait and 5-year benefit period.

> **Wayne and Vicki** have already retired. They have started to live on their combined super funds. We have cancelled all insurances for them as they are now in retirement and have no debts. The cost of insurance at this age is prohibitive.

While insurance can seem overwhelming, especially with complex family dynamics and various investments, it's an essential part of financial planning. Remember, you're not alone in the process. A financial planner can help you navigate the industry jargon and policy options and will be there to guide you through the process, making decisions easier.

Remember, the only thing that will stop you from achieving financial certainty is if you don't have an income. Don't be part of the 44% of Australians living without income cover.[10] Protect your present lifestyle and secure your future with the right insurances for you. And when doing your yearly goal setting don't forget to take a look at your insurance policies and ensure the sum insured is still the correct amount for you.

The Grim Reality

Life can be unpredictable. And when it is, it often catches us off-guard, particularly if we haven't adequately prepared. It's crucial to think about what could happen if you don't have insurance in place and a plan for the worst-case scenario. 2 in 5 Australians will contract cancer in their life.[11] In 2022, an estimated 3% of Australia had coronary heart disease at some time in their lives.[12]

In the earlier chapters we met Vicki and Wayne. Let's delve a little deeper into their backstory. Well, it's really more Vicki's story than Wayne's. At the age of 31, Vicki had a home, a thriving career and a nest egg for her future. Then, her world turned upside down in the space of a few hours as she was driving home and her car spun out into another vehicle with two children in it. One of those children ended up in hospital for a very long time.

In the blink of an eye, Vicki found herself in a legal battle with her vehicle's manufacturers and the driver of the other car. The legal fight drained her financially and her nest egg vanished. The concussion from the accident also cost Vicki her job, and her confidence crumbled.

At this point, Vicki met Wayne and they married. She worked part-time while raising their children, which was right for them. Vicki's story underscores one vital point: protecting the wealth you have is critically important.

At 31 you might easily argue that there's still plenty of time to recover from such a situation. But having income cover would have been a lifeline for Vicki during that time and well into the future. It would have helped with the medical issues resulting from the concussion and the lost income for that year. Yet, at 31, like many young people, Vicki felt invincible. She had car and home insurance but didn't realise she might need more.

The importance of cover

This isn't about pushing you into more insurance. However, in my work I see people every day who never thought to protect the things that mattered and have ended up in a situation where insurance might have made a significant difference. No-one thinks anything will happen to them, but cancer and so many health-related issues don't discriminate. As I tell my clients, we can craft a detailed retirement plan, but if illness or an accident strikes and work is no longer an option, where will the income come from? Insurance protects this and ensures you'll reach your retirement goals no matter what happens.

Think about it like this: income cover as a rule of thumb only 2% of gross income and is fully tax-deductible. It's a small price to pay for peace of mind in the event of an illness or accident.

If you still have doubts about the importance of insurance, consider the case of one of our clients who worked in retail. Unfortunately, he passed away unexpectedly in his late thirties. He had a $2,000,000 life cover policy in place to ensure his debts would be paid out and his wife and children would be supported in case anything happened to him. This situation shows exactly why advice is so important. His wife didn't need to resort to financial help or fundraising pages to cover the funeral costs and time off work, something I sadly see far too often.

We currently have a long-standing client, Tony, who is battling motor neurone disease. Tony has worked all his life, and without loss of income cover that provides $8,500 per month income in lieu until he is 65, his family would be facing a challenging situation. Tony also has life cover and will receive this payout once he is given the prognosis of having fewer than 2 years to live, allowing him to spend quality time with his wife and kids. Tony's $100,000 trauma insurance was a great help with medical costs and mortgage payments.

More examples

Clive, a young lawyer, was hesitant to take our advice to have $1,000,000 life and TPD cover, and $100,000 of trauma and income cover. He felt he was too young to need so much coverage. I worked closely with Clive and after 10 phone calls and emails I convinced him to take out the required cover to help his family, just in case. Sadly, at 38, Clive suffered a minor stroke 2 years after we took out this cover.

Although he returned to work after two weeks, he found he could no longer concentrate. His $1,000,000 payout allowed him to pay off his mortgage and other debts at the time. He was also receiving an income benefit of $15,000 per month. Over time, Clive became a lecturer and was doing well until a massive stroke took his life in his mid-forties. Thankfully, his remaining life cover paid out another $1,000,000 to his family.

Clive's story is a reminder of the importance of sufficient insurance coverage. It can provide the needed financial cushion when the unexpected happens, giving you and your family time to regroup and plan the next steps without the additional stress of financial worries.

• • •

A number of years ago, I worked closely with a dentist who also happened to be a good friend of mine. Bill had a disabled son from a previous marriage. I advised him to put in place $2,000,000 worth of life insurance, but due to the cost and his age (mid-forties at the time), he reduced it to $1.5 million.

Tragically, when Bill died in his early fifties, his second wife received the entire $1.5 million pay-out plus all the other assets from the estate. His son ended up with nothing. The situation was heartbreaking to witness, but it underscores the importance of acting sooner rather than later when it comes to financial planning. Part of our process at Virtual Financial Advice is to ensure not only the insurance is taken care of, but also the binding nominations, the estate planning including a will and Powers of Attorney. If Bill had put this in place, his son could have been looked after as per his wishes.

It starts with you

Remember, it begins with you making an effort. Dedicate one day per year to concentrate on all your financial affairs including tax, estate planning, insurances, loans and debt levels. Look for better interest rates, best deals on insurance premiums and investments and consider whether you should buy an investment property or start a share portfolio.

Don't be like Bill. Always make sure you actually get around to it. Life is unpredictable, and you never know when your time will come. Ensure your will has been done professionally, which we will discuss in detail later on. Check that you have an appropriate level of life and trauma cover in place. Ask yourself: if you had to take sustained time off work for treatment, would your income be covered?

Consider prenuptial agreements, inheritance planning, tax planning and other protective measures. Protecting what you have and the people you care about might mean investing more time in complex family structures like Ant and Emily's, but it's worth getting it right.

Remember, having the right cover in place can make a world of difference when the unthinkable happens. It doesn't just give you financial security; it gives choices to those left behind. It takes away the financial stress, leaving them to focus on dealing with the personal loss.

Take the time now to plan for the future. Secure the financial safety and peace of mind for yourself and your loved ones. After all, the grim reality is that not having a plan can have far-reaching consequences that could have been avoided with the right foresight and planning.

I think it's really important to take time out to look at your financial affairs. I often give the example of a home loan; the bank is not going to ring you and ask if you want a lower interest rate. But a number of my clients have saved thousands of dollars and taken years off their loan by taking the time and ringing their bank to ask whether their current rate is the best on offer. All banks have a retention team, and they will try to keep you if you a great client and always make your repayments on time.

Whether it's Vicki and Wayne, Tony, Clive or Bill, each of these stories drives home the same point: advice pays. It's not just about the money, it's about ensuring that if the worst were to happen, you and your loved ones aren't left in a financial hole. Insurance isn't just another expense; it's a shield that protects you and your family from the financial impact of unexpected life events. It's about providing you with the peace of mind that comes from knowing that if anything were to happen to you, your loved ones would be financially secure.

Take the time now to review your insurance cover and financial plans. Speak to a professional and make sure that if the unexpected happens you are ready. In my opinion there is no excuse, life cover for $1,000,000 can be as little as buying a morning coffee. If you have 2 coffees a day, give one up! Remember, protecting your future starts today. Don't wait until it's too late. Plan now and give yourself the peace of mind you deserve.

ACTIVITY

Now is a great time to put this book down and do a bit of forecasting and consider what the worst-case scenario would be for you and your family if something happens and you have no insurance in place. Here is a list of possibilities to get you started:

Home Loan $____________ per month

Living Expenses $____________ per month

Education $____________ per month

Medical Expenses $____________ per month

If you have to live on Jobseeker payments, the average allowance for a couple is $631.20 per fortnight. Does this cover your expenses?[13]

Unravelling the Magic of Budgeting: Your Key to a Stress-Free Retirement

The word 'budget' often carries a somewhat gloomy connotation, a bit like 'diet'. But it's all about perspective. Much like a healthy diet and regular exercise pave the way to physical wellbeing, a well-managed budget is your ticket to financial fitness. So, roll up your sleeves and let's make friends with budgeting!

Budgeting: more than just crunching numbers

You see, a budget isn't just about keeping track of every dollar and cent (though that's certainly part of it). It's about understanding where your money is going, identifying opportunities to save and, most importantly, gaining control over your financial future. Having a degree of control and understanding the ins and outs of your finances will play a big part in reaching your goals.

I personally believe in doing a budget but not letting it depress you; the goal with the budget is to work out how you are tracking. If you have a shortfall you have to choose whether to earn more money (my preference) or cut out some bills. A great tool to use is the Budget planner on the moneysmart website: **https://moneysmart.gov.au/budgeting/budget-planner**

Know where your money goes: tracking your income and expenses

Let's start with the basics. A budget is simply a plan that outlines what you expect to earn (income) and spend (expenses) over a set period, often a month, but this will often largely depend on your pay cycle.

The first step in budgeting is to track all of these, even that morning coffee you grab on your way to work. Some people love to use an app to do this, others prefer the good old excel spreadsheet. There is no right or wrong way to track your spending so use whatever format works best for you. The only important thing is being consistent and honest with yourself.

With my clients we talk about doing a yearly planning of cash flow, this allocates how much should be transferred to your spending account each pay period. If you only spend the amount allocated there won't be a problem. Another way of tracking this is to use an offset account and a visa card. All of your pay goes into the offset account, and you pay off your credit card monthly. You just need to be disciplined on how much you allow in your yearly budget.

There are alternatives like MyBudget that tracks all of your expenses and are very strict on how you spend your money. However, I prefer the yearly budget with using the offset account. I pay all expenses on visa, and this also helps with holidays as the card accumulates points.

Categorise your spending

Once you have this data, categorise your expenses. Common categories might include groceries, utilities, housing, entertainment, transport, health and savings. You might be surprised to find out just how much you're spending on take away, or how those online purchases add up. Don't be too hard on yourself though; we're here to understand and learn, not to judge! When I started looking at my budget I realised how much I spent on dining out, which is a favourite luxury of mine. I then cut this back to date night and one other night out. You just need to find what works for you. I believe if the budget doesn't add up you may need to find another revenue stream.

Make your money work for you

Prioritise your spending

Now, you need to review these categories and decide where you can make changes, if necessary. Prioritise essential needs over wants. Sure, we all enjoy a good meal out, but cooking at home more often might be the financial equivalent of hitting the gym: it might require some effort, but it's good for you and your wallet!

Set financial goals

Next, you want to set some financial goals. Are you aiming for an early retirement? Looking to pay off your mortgage sooner? Want to take a dream vacation? These goals will help shape your budget, and trust me, there's a sweet sense of satisfaction when you see yourself making progress towards these targets.

The connection to retirement

Now you might be wondering, what does all this have to do with retirement? Well, a lot actually! In many cases in retirement, we need to take out an annuity to help us qualify for the aged pension. Getting the pension, however small it may be, can lead to a lot of benefits including discounted medical fees with a health-care card as well as discounted electricity bills and rates bills. So, a budget of how much you spend will help you in setting the annuity. We will cover this in greater detail in the chapter on retirement.

In summary, budgeting will help with the following:

- **Understanding your needs:** Your current budget can give you a snapshot of your expected expenses and income to help set goals for the future. A great goal is to pay off the home loan or make extra contributions into super.
- **Planning for retirement:** The more you save now, the more you'll have for your retirement. A well-planned budget will allow you to save more effectively. It will help to calculate what type and size annuity you should consider.
- **Reducing stress:** When you're in control of your finances, you worry less. Less stress means a happier you, both now and in retirement. Financial stress is a major cause for family breakdowns, divorces and health related issues. It's amazing the difference a budget combined with a financial and retirement plan can do.
- **Create investments:** The right budgeting helps create wealth and once you get on top of this the next step is to look at the equity you have built up. If you are on top of cashflow and you have equity in your home, an investment property, share portfolio or an MDA can be a great way to invest for the future.

This is budgeting in a nutshell and at Virtual Financial Advice we take our clients through budgeting in a comprehensive way utilising our checklists. Remember, budgeting isn't about depriving yourself of joys today but ensuring you can enjoy those joys long into the future. With a budget in hand, you're not only ready to face the present, but you're also well-equipped to embrace your retirement future.

PART FIVE

Debt Management and Reduction

Debt Management

It is impossible to write a book about retirement planning without also addressing the matter of debt. Let's face it, we all have to deal with debt at some point in our lives and it's important to understand the difference between good debt and bad debt. We'll get to the 'good' debt later. But first, let's look at the matter of getting out of being in debt, so that you can free up more resources for developing and sticking to a great retirement plan.

Debt is one thing that can keep you up at night and cause challenges in every aspect of your life. Debt management is the process of creating a plan to repay outstanding debts in a timely and efficient manner. It can involve negotiating with creditors to lower interest rates or monthly payments, or consolidating multiple debts into one manageable payment. The goal of debt management is to improve your financial situation and reduce the stress associated with overwhelming debt.

One of the first steps in debt management is to identify all outstanding debts, including credit card balances, loans and unpaid bills. Once all debts have been identified, prioritise them by interest rate, with the highest interest rate debts being paid off first. This is because high-interest rate debts will cost more in the long run and should be eliminated as soon as possible.

One strategy for debt management is to consolidate multiple debts into one manageable payment. This can be done through a balance transfer credit card, a personal loan or a home equity loan. By consolidating debts, you are able to simplify your monthly payments and can often secure a lower interest rate. However, it's important to note that consolidation loans typically require a good credit score to qualify and may require collateral.

When consolidating your debts you also have to be wary that the bank will reset the loan at 30 years; if you're over 50 this is not ideal. The brokers and the banks do this to help the client qualify for the loan. Getting advice is important as we would then ensure you are paying loan repayments that will have the loan paid out at retirement or a strategy to ensure it is paid out, this can include downsizing, using super funds or inheritance.

Another strategy for debt management is to negotiate with creditors to lower interest rates or monthly payments. This can be done by contacting the creditor directly and explaining your financial situation. Creditors may be willing to work with you to create a more manageable payment plan.

As mentioned previously, creating a budget is key. Building an emergency fund is also important, as it can provide a financial cushion in case of unexpected expenses.

Overall, debt management is an important step in improving your financial situation and reducing the stress associated with overwhelming debt. By identifying outstanding debts, prioritising them, consolidating them, negotiating with creditors, creating a budget and building an emergency fund, individuals can take control of their debt and improve their financial future.

Here's a simple 10 step checklist for debt management:

1. **Identify all outstanding debts:** Make a list of all credit card balances, loans and unpaid bills.

2. **Prioritise debts:** Order the debts by interest rate, with the highest interest rate debts being paid off first.

3. **Create a budget:** Identify areas of unnecessary spending and cut back on them to free up money for debt repayment.

4. **Consolidate debts:** Consider consolidating multiple debts into one manageable payment through a balance transfer credit card, personal loan or home equity loan. This is one of the main strategies we use as most people have gained equity over the last 5 years, and this gives us a great opportunity to consolidate into one debt.

5. **Negotiate with creditors:** Contact creditors directly to explain your financial situation and ask for lower interest rates or monthly payments.

6. **Make a plan:** Develop a plan for repaying debts, including a timeline and a budget for each debt.

7. **Automate payments:** Set up automatic payments to ensure that debts are paid on time and to avoid late fees.

8. **Monitor credit reports:** Keep an eye on credit reports to ensure that debts are being reported accurately and to check for any fraudulent activity.

9. **Seek professional help:** If the debt is overwhelming, seek help from a financial adviser or credit counsellor. There is free support available:
   - **National Debt Helpline:** A free, confidential service that provides financial counselling to individuals and families

facing debt problems. The helpline operates from 9.30am to 4.30pm, Monday to Friday (1800 007 008).

- **Small Business Debt Helpline:** If you are a small business owner facing debt difficulties, the Small Business Debt Helpline (1800 413 828) can provide support.
- **Mob Strong Debt Helpline:** For Aboriginal and Torres Strait Islander people, the Mob Strong Debt Helpline (1800 808 488) provides financial counselling.
- **Moneysmart.gov.au:** This website offers a wealth of information on managing debt and finances.

10. **Build an emergency fund:** Having an emergency fund can help avoid accruing more debt in case of unexpected expenses.

Good debt for investment purposes

Good debt, also known as 'investment debt', is debt that is used to purchase assets that will increase in value over time. This type of debt can be a valuable investment strategy for building wealth and achieving financial goals.

One of the most common forms of good debt is a mortgage. When used to purchase an investment property, a mortgage can be a good debt because the value of the property is likely to increase over time. Additionally, the interest paid on an investment mortgage is tax-deductible, which can help to lower the overall cost of the debt.

Another example of good debt is taking out a loan to invest in a business. A business loan can provide the necessary capital to start or expand a business, which can lead to increased income and potential long-term growth.

Student loans can also be considered good debt, as they are often used to invest in one's education, which can lead to higher-paying job opportunities and increased earning potential.

It is important to note that not all debt is good debt. Credit card debt, for example, is considered bad debt because it is often used to purchase depreciating assets such as consumer goods, and the interest rates are usually high. Buying a motor vehicle is bad debt as motor vehicles drop in value very quickly.

When considering taking on good debt, it's important to have a solid plan for repayment and to be sure that the investment will generate enough income to repay the debt. Additionally, it's important to have an emergency fund in place to provide a financial cushion in case of unexpected expenses. I normally consider three months income or wages to be a great start, and this should be set aside in your offset account.

• • •

In conclusion, good debt, used in the right way, can be a valuable investment strategy for building wealth. It's important to understand the difference between good and bad debt, have a solid repayment plan and ensure that the investment will generate enough income to repay the debt. With proper planning and management, good debt can be a powerful tool in achieving financial goals. Remember, always repay bad debt first like credit cards, personal loans and motor vehicle loans.

Debt Recycling

This can be quite useful in paying off debts in the long term, the strategy uses investment such as shares and or property to payoff the home loan in a faster term

There are 4 areas we look at:

1. Debt analysis where we look at the current debt and see if we can restructure loan or reduce interest rate a reduction

of .4% on a $800k loan will reduce the loan term from 30 years to 27 years a 3 year difference

2. Additional mortgage payments of $500pm saves 8 years in loan repayments

3. Investment portfolio of $1000 pm will save 9 years in loan repayments

4. Debt recycling will save up to 11 years in loan repayments

ACTIVITY

Now is a great time to put this book down and calculate your debts:

Credit Card Debt ____________ Interest Rate __________

Home Loan _________________ Interest Rate __________

Investment Loan _____________ Interest Rate __________

Car Loan ____________________ Interest Rate __________

Other _______________________ Interest Rate __________

PART SIX

Retirement Planning

What Does Retirement Look Like for You?

Now that you have an understanding of the retirement-asset landscape, it is time to do some visualisation. Close your eyes, sit back and let your imagination run wild for a few minutes.

If you could create the most perfect retirement, what exactly would It look like?

Retirement planning is the favourite part of my work I love being able show clients how they can retire using not only their money but government money and benefits.

Depending on what your age and stage of life currently is, your future retirement might look different now compared to 10 years ago, or even in 10-years' time. But as we've discussed, it's good to have a solid conversation with your partner (or yourself) to really see if you're aiming for the same things or even have goals set. It's also good to know what the possibilities might be for you. Could you actually become a paperback novelist or get paid to write a travel guide as you hit your 70s? Might that investment decision you make now mean you can just do some university papers for fun or a university degree you've always wanted to do once you've retired from work? Can you picture yourself restoring old cars, building a boat, taking up sailing, marathons, train journeys, flipping houses, teaching your grandkids to swim, baking or gardening? Let your imagination run free.

Also consider what age do you wish to retire? At Virtual Financial we use the latest state-of-the-art software to show our clients where they are today and how that will look in the future. We take into consideration superannuation contributions, employer contributions and your own contribution. We then set returns at 6% to give us a guide; we always use a lower figure to be sure we achieve our goal. Our current MDA, for example, has achieved a 9% return. We then take into consideration insurance expenses paid by super and lastly any lump sums to be paid in as a result of asset sale or an inheritance.

The retirement planner is presented in a graph for our clients as well as the raw data so they can see what figures we have used to chart the retirement plan. We show them where they will be with respect to their own money, as well as the added benefit of the Age Pension. We have so many clients who say that they didn't think they were on track but are now equipped with the knowledge that they can retire comfortably. One of the biggest issues most clients have in retirement is making sure that when they stop working, they have enough to enjoy the rest of their life without stress.

It's easy to get stressed over things the media headlines and reporting. We've currently got rising interest rates and though some of us have lived through years with some high interest rates (17% in the 1980s) most people under 30 don't remember these times. The cost of living is also increasing at a steady rate and that's probably where concerns come into play for many people.

The big questions we ask our clients when we start to set retirement goals are:

- How much income do you need to comfortably live in retirement? The Association of Superannuation Funds of Australia (AFSA) states that $73,077 is needed for a couple and $51,805 is needed for a single for a comfortable lifestyle (at time of writing).[14]
- Do you have enough super and or other assets like selling down an investment property?
- What do you need to do to achieve your retirement plan? Do you need to start making extra personal contributions or salary sacrifice?

The very first thing you need to do is have that meeting with a qualified financial planner. Firms like ours provide the first meeting free of charge so there is no excuse to not get initial advice. We start the process by having you complete our questionnaires: the Financial Health check and the All About You questionnaire. Then you will speak with a professional investment and financial planning expert about your situation, your own needs and what your expectations are. This will give you a tailored response to your individual circumstances and needs, saving you a lot of time filtering through broad advice online. So, talking with an expert is likely to save you a lot of time, anxiety and probably make a big difference to your back pocket at the end of the day too. We had a client recently who was able to see how they could generate an extra $145,000 over a 10-year period by purely using annuities and a strategy to get government benefits.

Let's talk about lifestyle

It's very hard to put a number on how much you need to fund your lifestyle because it depends on whether you're a single person or in a couple, the type of lifestyle you're used to, and your age and stage in life.

Our sample case studies will all have a different line of thought about this, how much they want to draw down from their super and from their government pension each year. Part of our process as financial advisers is to work through these points of reference.

NOTE: for all of the following dollar amounts we'll be using today's Australian dollar as a guide, because it's too hard to predict what the actual amounts will be in the future.

If we work backwards to an income expectation of around $70,000 per year for retirement living, you'll arrive at the figure you'll need to start with. It's important to note the huge misconception that you need over $3,000,000 to achieve that. You don't. We have a lot of clients retiring on $500,000 and retiring quite comfortably because if you have less than $900,000 worth of other assets, you're able to access the Age Pension as well. So, you're able to use government money plus your own money which means the 'nest egg' may not need to be as high as you'd think.

Many people are quite shocked when they find out they are actually on track if they get to under $1,000,000 in retirement savings. Or that they may be able to retire earlier than they had thought. Obviously, there's a lot of strategies that go behind the planning. Some people in their mid-50s are closer to being able to retire at 60 than they may have ever though.

So, what is the amount you need in retirement? A rule of thumb is that you need two-thirds of your pre-retirement income. However, when we do your retirement plan, we use the latest software that also includes what you will get from the Age Pension as well as using your superannuation. I have worked out what you need based on owning your home after paying off your mortgage. The Association of Superannuation Funds of Australia estimate the following:

To retire as a couple at 67 and to last until age 100 on $77,077 per annum, you need $690,000 in today's dollars. As a single person to retire comfortably you need $51,805 per annum you need $595,000.[15] As we are also using government money to draw down, not just your own, please see the graph below.[16]

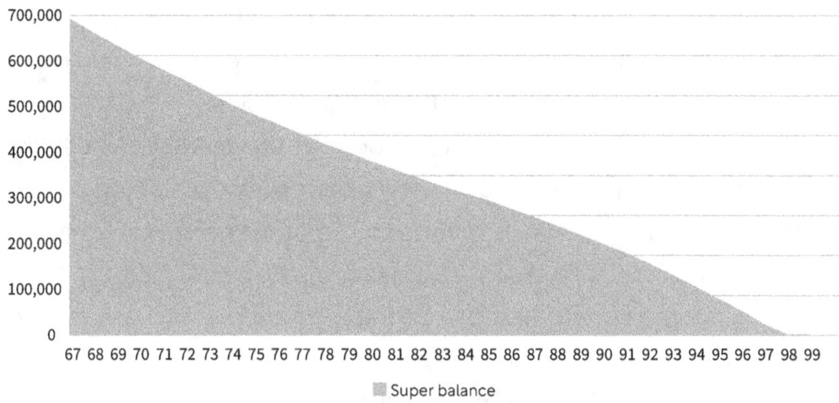

Why the government only focusses on fees

One secret that government or industry funds won't tell you about is annuities. They are like a term deposit but come with pension benefits. In most circumstances they only account for 60% of your asset test, which unlike super and other investments, which account for 100%, at age 84, they only account for 30% of the asset test.

What's a lifetime annuity?

This is a financial product that pays you a guaranteed income stream for the rest of your life. It is similar to a term deposit but has other features such as reversionary pension, which means the Annuity is transferred to your partner upon your death.

This is a great product to give certainty to your retirement goals. It also has Services Australia benefits as only 60% is included for age pension calculations when calculating your government pension.

The annuity can also be indexed to keep up with inflation We use Challenger for our Annuities who hold considerable market share.[17]

We use annuities all the time with our clients. What we normally do with an annuity is we work out what our client's fixed costs are for the year. Let's just say their total expenses normally come to around $20,000 per annum. We set up an annuity for whatever figure that needs to be to ensure that they have that $20,000 come into their account every year for the rest of their life. This also helps to get them under the government threshold of income so they can receive concession cards that come with the Age Pension.

This way, regardless of what happens in the markets, you'll know that you're going to get that annuity paid every year. And the best part about it, as a couple, it reverts to the other person on death. So, for the rest of their life, their expenses are paid for. Annuity is used to have an income stream that can be indexed and paid to you and your partner for the rest of your life.

It's essentially like a term deposit: very safe and it's guaranteed income for life. So, it's a great vehicle to use for Services Australia purposes when you are applying for the pension.

Now you wouldn't be using an annuity unless you can cover a certain amount of expenses. Generally an annuity around $100,000 would be the minimum amount we would use this way.

A lot of Australians don't get simple retirement planning advice because they are advised not to by industry fund operators. But you don't know what you don't know and if financial planning is something you don't have the means or desire to learn about extensively, then get some real advice from an independent expert. I saved a client (who was in an industry super fund) $150,000 by having a simple structure, a plan and the means to implement that plan. That's a lot of money to save when you're talking about retirement funds.

The age of retirement in Australia

With your own super fund and pension, you can retire at 60. But you are not eligible for the Age Pension until you turn 67. So, building your retirement around the age of 60 means that for the first seven years you would need to use only your own money. However, you can still apply for senior concession cards at 65. In general terms, you can have up to roughly $900,000 of other assets on top of your house and still receive a concession card. So, if your assets are in excess of that amount, we need to work on strategies, such as annuities, to ensure you are eligible for concession cards. They can be more beneficial than you may think. The benefits of a concessional cards can include cheaper prescriptions, transport and discount on water rates and discounts on insurances

Real Life Examples: How our clients see their retirement

Kieran and Caitlin are young, so retirement is a long way off. However, the more you plan now the easier it is in retirement. Caitlin works in the public service, which is ideal due to higher super contributions. We recommend boosting super to 15% through salary sacrificing. As Kieran works for a private business, making his own salary sacrifice contributions can really help. We would normally recommend this once they have purchased their first home.

Nic and Talisha are in their mid-30s and have their first home. They are now in a position to consider salary sacrificing, however if they are to have more kids they may wait until after both Nick and Talisha are back to work after parental leave and there is enough cash flow for salary sacrificing.

Joe and Mark have no kids and are both working full-time, so are in the perfect position to maximise their super contributions. Setting up a SMSF and really working their super with an MDA to help them grow their wealth in a risk-adjusted way is the best strategy.

Karen is single so getting retirement right is very important. 80% of retirees are concerned that their income in retirement will not last. Having the right portfolio and contribution strategy is very important. Salary sacrificing would be a great option.

Ant and Emily are approaching retirement, so the priority should be to ensure a retirement plan is done and reviewed each year as well as maximising their super contributions. Advice at this stage of their lives is critical. They may also consider the downsizing contribution strategy in retirement as well as small business concessions into super. Topping up super with maximum contributions is ideal.

Wayne and Vicki have already retired and need to ensure they are maximising their Age Pension. It is important that they have applied for concession cards and have invested in an annuity that will give them certainty over their retirement.

ACTIVITY

Now is a great time to put this book down and download the checklist from our website ***https://virtualfinancial.com.au/*** *and take the time to fill in all the answers to gain an insight into what you want your retirement to look like.*

Balancing the equation with investments

When it comes to how much you can invest while still being eligible for the Age Pension, there isn't a hard and fast rule. Remember, Services Australia considers your income, as well as your assets, to determine your pension entitlement. Any income you earn from your investments will factor into this.

The key lies in striking a balance. If you are considering balancing your super savings with the age pension you will want to have enough investments to provide a decent income and maintain your lifestyle, but not so much that they negatively impact your pension. This balancing act might sound like a tightrope walk, but that's where financial planning expertise can be so valuable.

Social security

<table>
<tr><th colspan="5">Age Pension rates</th></tr>
<tr><td></td><td colspan="2">Fortnightly</td><td colspan="2">Annual</td></tr>
<tr><td>Single</td><td colspan="2">$1,144.40</td><td colspan="2">$29,754.40</td></tr>
<tr><td>Couple combined</td><td colspan="2">$1,725.20</td><td colspan="2">$44,855.20</td></tr>
<tr><td>Illness separated combined</td><td colspan="2">$2,288.80</td><td colspan="2">$59,508.80</td></tr>
<tr><td colspan="5">Includes Pension and Energy Supplement</td></tr>
<tr><th colspan="5">Pension Asset Test</th></tr>
<tr><td></td><td colspan="2">For full pension</td><td colspan="2">Disqualifying limits</td></tr>
<tr><td colspan="5">Homeowners</td></tr>
<tr><td>Single</td><td colspan="2">$314,000</td><td colspan="2">$695,500</td></tr>
<tr><td>Couple combined</td><td colspan="2">$470,000</td><td colspan="2">$1,045,500</td></tr>
<tr><td>Illness separated</td><td colspan="2">$470,000</td><td colspan="2">$1,233,000</td></tr>
<tr><td colspan="5">Non-homeowners</td></tr>
<tr><td>Single</td><td colspan="2">$566,000</td><td colspan="2">$947,500</td></tr>
<tr><td>Couple combined</td><td colspan="2">$722,000</td><td colspan="2">$1,297,500</td></tr>
<tr><td>Illness separated</td><td colspan="2">$722,000</td><td colspan="2">$1,485,000</td></tr>
<tr><th colspan="5">Pension Income Test</th></tr>
<tr><td></td><td colspan="2">For full pension</td><td colspan="2">Disqualifying limits</td></tr>
<tr><td></td><td>Fortnightly</td><td>Annual</td><td>Fortnightly</td><td>Annual</td></tr>
<tr><td>Single</td><td>$212</td><td>$5,512</td><td>$2,500.80</td><td>$65,020.80</td></tr>
<tr><td>Couple combined</td><td>$372</td><td>$9,672</td><td>$3,822.40</td><td>$99,382.40</td></tr>
<tr><td>Illness separated</td><td>$372</td><td>$9,672</td><td>$4,949.60</td><td>$128,689.60</td></tr>
</table>

Source: Challenger Fast Facts[18]

Understanding Australian Retirement Assets and the Pension

Our financial life can be quite complex and intertwined. Whether it's understanding our assets or figuring out the government pension eligibility, everything ties back to our ultimate dream of a worry-free, comfortable retirement. So, let's break down these complexities together, making them easy to understand and, believe it or not, somewhat enjoyable!

The ins and outs of retirement assets

Firstly, let's understand what the Australian Government considers as your 'assets'. Broadly speaking, an asset is anything you own that holds financial value. In the context of retirement, Services Australia (the Australian Government's provider of social security benefits) classifies your assets into two categories: assessable and non-assessable. What follows is a brief outline and is in no way a complete list.

Assessable assets

These are the assets that Centrelink will take into account when assessing your eligibility for the Age Pension. They include:

- **Financial investments:** This covers a wide range of investments such as term deposits, shares, managed funds, superannuation (if you're over Age Pension age), and money you have loaned to other people.
- **Property assets:** This is not your family home, but any additional real estate you own. So, if you have an investment property or a holiday home, it's included here.
- **Personal assets:** This could be anything from cars and boats to home contents and personal effects.
- **Business assets:** If you're still running a small business in retirement, assets associated with that business count too.

Non-assessable assets

Now, here's some good news. Some assets don't count towards your Age Pension assets test. The most notable of these is your principal home (the house you live in most of the time). Certain pre-paid funeral investments and some types of life insurance policies are also exempt.

The assets test

The assets test is one of the ways Centrelink determines your eligibility for the Age Pension. Essentially, it's a sliding scale. The more assets you have, the less pension you might receive. Once your assets exceed a certain value, known as the assets test limit, you will no longer be eligible to receive any Age Pension. It is important to note that the requirements for this test can change, and this should be used as a guide only.

The assets test limit cut off in July 2024 for a single homeowner was $686,250 while for a couple who are homeowners, it was $1,031,000. Don't forget to check the latest figures as they do change over time.

Balancing the equation with investments

When it comes to how much you can invest while still being eligible for the government pension, there isn't a hard and fast rule. Remember, Centrelink considers your income, as well as your assets, to determine your pension entitlement. Any income you earn from your investments will factor into this.

The key lies in striking a balance. If you are considering balancing your super savings with the Age Pension, you will want to have enough investments to provide a decent income and maintain your lifestyle, but not so much that they negatively impact your Age Pension. This balancing act might sound like a tightrope walk, but that's where financial planning expertise can be so valuable. We recommend giving assets to your family as up to $30,000 can be gifted over 5 years, to consider doing any renovations to the family home, and a funeral bond of $15,000 each before applying for the pension. Be careful what you value other personal assets at, for example your home and contents are not the value you purchased them for but what you could see them being worth in a couple of weeks. We also do work with annuities that only account for 60% of your pension in most cases. Getting advice is critical in this area. The number one benefit is getting hold of the pension card. In Queensland, we have great incentives including discount water and council rates and pharmaceutical benefits.

• • •

Remember, this is a complex area, and it's easy to feel like you're navigating a maze. But that's where we, your financial planning guides, step in. We'll help you map out a clear path, taking into account your assets, investments and potential pension, so that your retirement journey feels more like a leisurely walk in the park rather than a precarious tightrope walk.

ACTIVITY

Now is a great time to take out the pen and paper and list all the assessable assets you have at this current time.

Shares

....

....

Cash Savings including term deposits

....

....

Investment property

....

....

Superannuation balance

....

....

Cars, boats, caravan

....

....

Home and contents

....

....

PART SEVEN

Estate Planning

The Importance of Having an Enduring Power of Attorney

Understanding Powers of Attorney: General vs Enduring

One essential aspect of planning your future is Powers of Attorney and the vital role they play. What most of us don't understand is the difference between a General Power of Attorney and an Enduring Power of Attorney, and where these important documents can support you and your loved ones in times of need. Unfortunately, the laws in Australia are not uniform and each state and territory each has their own specific requirements as to the drafting and execution of the powers.

General Power of Attorney

Imagine you're going on a holiday, and you need someone to take care of your house, water the plants and collect the mail. You'd probably ask a friend or family member, someone you trust, to do this for you while your away. A General Power of Attorney is somewhat like that. It allows you to appoint a trusted person to make financial and legal decisions for you, but only for a specific time or under particular circumstances. Perhaps you'll be out of the country, or maybe you need assistance with a one-time event like selling a property. Once the situation changes, or the task is complete, the general power of attorney ends.

Enduring Power of Attorney

Now, consider that you want someone to look after your house indefinitely, if something were to happen to you that prevented you from managing things yourself. That's where an Enduring Power of Attorney comes in. Unlike the General Power of Attorney, it doesn't have an expiry date linked to a specific situation or your mental capacity. It 'endures' or continues even if you become unable to make decisions for yourself due to illness or accident.

An Enduring Power of Attorney (EPA) is a legal document that allows someone to appoint another person (either their attorney and/or trusted relative or spouse) to make decisions on their behalf if they become mentally incapacitated or otherwise unable to make decisions for themselves.

The 'attorney' or appointed EPA has the power to make decisions and manage your financial, property, personal care and welfare decisions if you become incapacitated. Unlike a regular Power of Attorney, which ceases to be valid if the person granting the power loses their mental capacity, an Enduring Power of Attorney remains valid even if the person granting the power becomes incapacitated. This document ensures that your appointed person can act on your behalf, aligning with your wishes and best interests.

Who's involved: the principal and the donee

The person granting the power is referred to as the principal, and the person who has been appointed is the attorney, also referred to as the donee. EPAs are set up in advance so action can be taken immediately. They cannot be set up with the principal is incapacitated, so it is vitally important to have this set up before you need it.

If you have an EPA set up, you can ensure someone you trust and who knows your wishes has the power to act on your behalf in the event of an accident. In the event that this hasn't been set up, next of kin status is often the fall-back position.

This is your safeguard, giving you peace of mind that your chosen person will have the legal authority to make crucial decisions on your behalf. Therefore, it is important to give very careful consideration to who you will appoint as your EPA. Whether it's a spouse, child or trusted friend, you need to feel confident they will adhere to your wishes.

Taking action: creating an EPA

The first step is deciding who to appoint, and if this will be more than one person. Some choose a spouse and trusted sibling, others a child. This can depend on the stage of life you are currently in.

I cannot state this enough: you simply never know in advance when you might need to have an EPA in place. This is not something that should only be considered relevant at some point in the future, but should be in place and updated as your life changes.

Taking the time to have an open and honest conversation with family or close friends about who should have this power is an important next step. No-one wants to think about the worst-case scenario but discussing this and your wishes beforehand can save your loved ones a lot of stress if they end up in that situation.

Consult a professional

Seeking advice from a legal or financial professional will ensure your EPA is correctly drafted and can be enacted in times of need. They will guide you through the process and answer any questions you have.

Life changes, and so should your EPA. Regular reviews and updates will make sure it continues to be relevant and reflect your wishes and circumstances. As you age you may want to change the EPA from your sibling to a child.

When an EPA is not in place

Should a person become incapacitated without an EPA, the process becomes complex and stressful. This is an extra burden for your loved ones when they are already grappling with huge decisions.

If the person who wishes to appoint an attorney (referred to as the 'principal') is already incapacitated, it is not possible for them to execute an Enduring Power of Attorney. In this case, an alternative option would be to apply for a court-appointed guardianship or administration order.

A guardianship order allows the court to appoint a guardian for the principal to make decisions about their personal care and welfare, while an administration order allows the court to appoint someone to manage the principal's financial and property affairs.

The process for obtaining a guardianship or administration order involves filing an application to the relevant court and may require the appointment of a medical practitioner to assess the incapacity of the principal. The court will also consider the views of any interested parties, such as family members, and will appoint a guardian or administrator that is considered to be in the best interests of the principal.

It's important to note that the process of obtaining a guardianship or administration order can be complex and time-consuming, and it is recommended to seek legal advice before proceeding.

An Enduring Power of Attorney is not just a legal formality; it's a vital part of planning for the unpredictable in life. An EPA can give us a degree of certainty that your wishes will be carried out in the worst-case scenario. It's about your care, your wishes and your control over who gets to make decisions when you can't.

Don't wait for a crisis to act, take the time to talk with your loved ones, consult your attorney and set the documents in place.

ACTIVITY

- **Decide who to appoint:** consider your spouse, child, or trusted friend.
- **Open and honest conversation:** discuss with your family or close friends who should have this power and your wishes.
- **Consult a professional:** legal or financial advisers will guide you through the process.
- **Regular reviews:** Life changes, and so should your EPA. Keep it updated to reflect your wishes.

The Importance of Having a Will

For many Australians, ensuring that their families are well taken care of after their passing is a significant concern. No matter what stage in life you are at, writing a will is an essential step in safeguarding your family. It starts with you; no one is going to do this for you, so why leave behind a mess for your loved ones? Yes, they might get the funds eventually, but having a will make this process a lot quicker, not to mention cheaper.

I once heard the expression that in estate planning, 3 things are crucial. That is making sure:

1. The right money
2. Goes to the right people
3. At the right time

Importantly, there are certain assets which may not form part of your estate that will need to be distributed via the will. Superannuation (unless the nomination notes the payment to the legal personal representative), certain life insurance policies and certain assets of a family trust may be such assets that might need to be dealt with separately.

I explain to all my clients that a will deals with how your assets that don't form part of superannuation are treated. With your super this is done with your nomination that can be binding or non-binding. A binding nomination means you have to have 2 witnesses; this is the preferred nomination we use.

So, if you have a will dealing with all your assets that are not in super and you have used a binding nomination within super, you are going to be well placed for your desires to be met.

Why write a will?

A will allows you to take control over the distribution of your assets after your death. You can ensure that your assets go exactly where you want them to. For those with children under 18, a will also specifies a guardian who will look after your children if you're no longer around.

Executors

Your executor is the person who ensures that you are buried/cremated according to your wishes and looks after your estate when you die. You can appoint up to four people to be executors of your estate. You can also appoint alternate executors in case any of your executors are unable or unwilling to act as your executors. If you are only appointing one executor, we strongly recommend that you also appoint an alternate executor.

How to write a will?

Making a will is not a difficult process and can be done is several ways:

Online services and software: Many platforms guide you through the process, offering both convenience and affordability. At Virtual Financial Advice we use Virtual Legal (No affiliation).

Appoint a lawyer: For those seeking a more personalised approach, a legal expert can ensure your will complies with all legal requirements and addresses all your wishes, this is especially important for clients that have businesses as they should also consider buy/sell agreements and to consider what will happen to their business on the event of death.

The essentials of writing a will

When creating a will, there are several things to consider. Firstly, you will need to list of the following:

- Property whether joint tenant or tenants in common
- All bank accounts including term deposits
- Investments including shares and investment properties
- Superannuation
- The beneficiaries of your superannuation (including whether this nomination is binding)
- Life insurance and the nominated beneficiary (if you have this type of insurance
- Family trust, if you have one, and the trustee, appointor/ principal, and a list of the beneficiaries.
- All assets and debts. Include everything

Once you have these details, you can:

- Decide how assets will be distributed. Think about who will inherit what and in what proportions.
- Name an executor. Select someone trustworthy to execute your will.

- Provisions for minor children. If applicable, appoint a guardian.
- Sign and store the will. It must be witnessed and kept in a safe place.
- Review and update regularly. As life changes, so should your will.

It's important to keep in mind that a will is a legal document and should be treated as such. Once the will is signed, it should be stored in a safe place, such as a safety deposit box, and the executor should be informed of its location. Additionally, it's important to review and update your will regularly, especially if your circumstances change. This can include marriage, divorce, the birth of children or significant changes in your assets, for example a large inheritance.

What happens if you don't have a will?

In the absence of a will, Queensland's state laws of intestacy apply. The challenges of this include:

- **Public Trustee Control:** dying intestate in Queensland might mean the Public Trustee takes control, potentially against your wishes.
- **Legal Costs:** your family may face expensive legal battles to reclaim control.
- **Distribution:** assets may be distributed in a way that doesn't reflect your personal wishes.

The consequences of dying without a will, intestacy, vary according to state and territory laws but what you can be sure of is your family and loved ones will have to fight for control at a time when they are grieving, adding to the emotional toll and burden of loss.

Writing a will might seem complex, but it's a crucial step to securing your family's future. Whether deciding who will care for your children or what happens to your home, these decisions are too vital to leave to chance. By drafting a will, you ensure that your loved ones are protected and grant yourself peace of mind.

An important website is https://www.willed.com.au/guides/how-do-the-rules-of-intestacy-vary-by-state-in-australia?srsltid=AfmBOook4pFaBFgo5lwAMc8qTcQSD5CeD2Zf2nWV6OppOGzxJBpLGhQP

Examples

I believe estate planning is very important, and I'm amazed at how many people do not have a will.

Research by Finder.com.au reveals most Australians don't have a will:

> *More than half of Australian adults don't have a will, even though it could mean their families are left out in the cold in the event of their death. Research has revealed 52% of us or 9.9 million Australians have not prepared the vital legal document. The survey found 34% of the population just haven't gotten around to it yet. Meanwhile, 14% said they didn't own enough assets or have enough wealth to justify the effort involved.*
>
> *Worryingly, 4% said they just don't want a will – even though dying without one could mean leaving loved ones in the lurch, as their estate would then be distributed solely according to intestacy law and not according to their wishes.*
>
> *If you die without making a valid will the implications are that your assets could be distributed in a way you would not have chosen.*[19]

Do you have a will?

State	Yes	No	Not sure
NSW	44%	52%	4%
QLD	50%	47%	3%
SA	42%	54%	4%
TAS	48%	52%	0%
VIC	41%	54%	5%
WA	45%	53%	2%

Source: finder.com.au survey of 2,011 Australians

An example of how Estate planning helped my client

Oscar, a client of mine, died unexpectedly from a motorcycle accident, however he had ensured his will was up to date and his family were looked after. The will ensured an easy and structured way to help his wife in difficult times. By being organised not only with the will, but with insurances and having all the boxes ticked, his wife was able to choose to stay at home and raise their kids. Without having a valid will and binding nomination you can cause a lot of financial stress on top of emotional stress.

Summary

Case Studies: An Overview

Throughout the chapters we took a deep dive into how I would advise our case studies and the actions they could take to help ensure their financial wellbeing. Hopefully you will have related to one of the examples and they have inspired you to start setting goals and planning for your financial future. What follows is an overview to keep you thinking.

Kieran and Caitlin

Kieran and Caitlin have just bought their first house and are on track to achieve financial freedom through investments and superannuation. My recommendation is to start an investment portfolio now and let it grow over the next 20 years. I have included the following wealth investment chart to show by only starting with $20,000, borrowing an additional $20,000 and investing $2,000 monthly how the compound effect works if you achieve a 10% return. In 10 years their net equity would be $528,000 and in 20 years their net equity would be $1,900,000. Keiran and Caitlin can also consider buying an investment property using their equity and using a debt recycling strategy to pay of their home at a faster rate

At their age, once they have built some equity, they could also look at an investment property to help with their wealth creation goal. Depending on their lifestyle they might not have the time or desire for an investment property and if this is the case then they can work on building their share portfolio.

Investment Plan

Cashflow projections (FV)

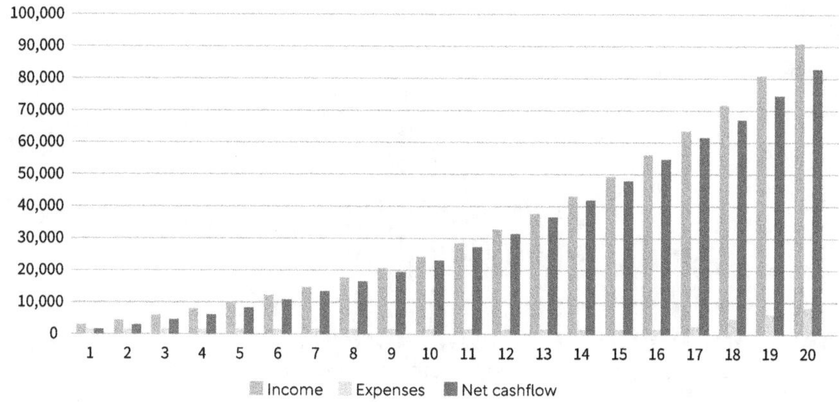

Capital projections (FV)

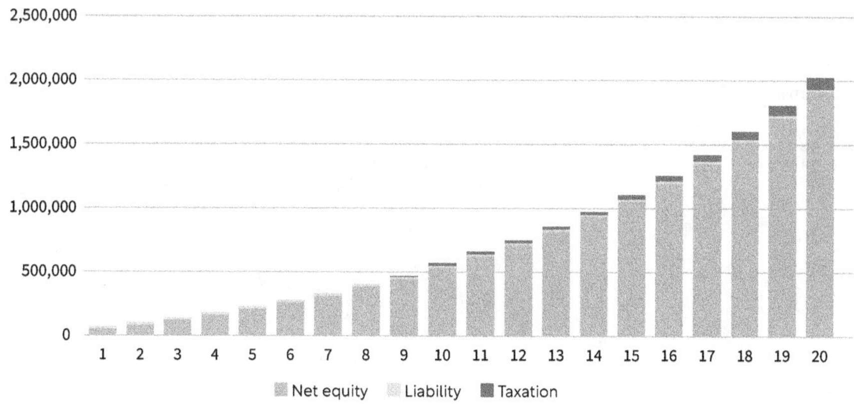

Retirement Plan

Projections

Cashflow

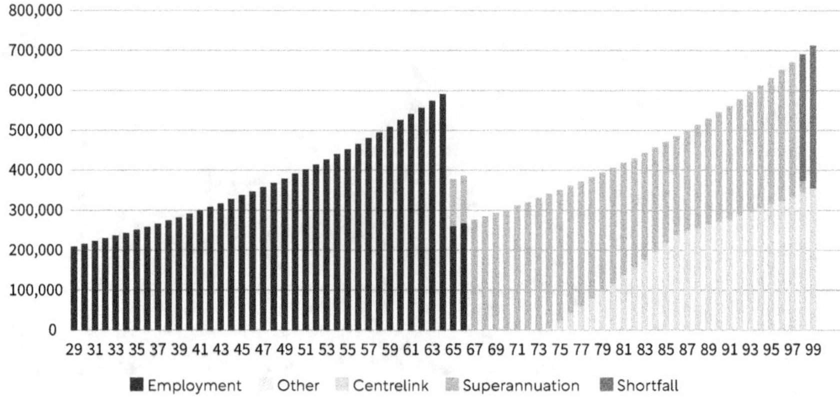

Super balance

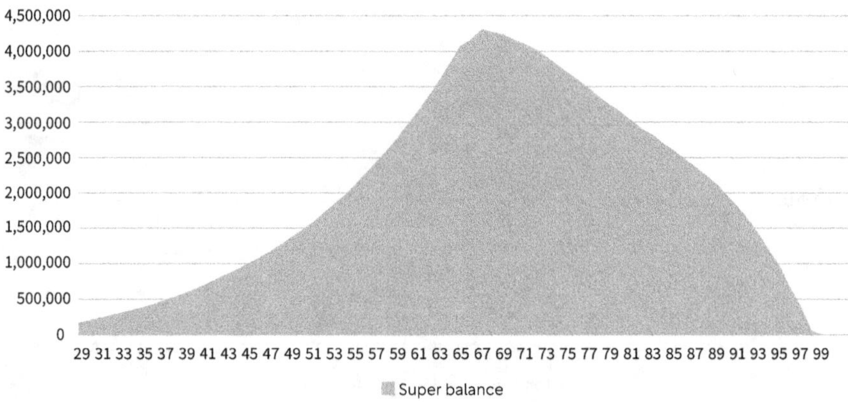

Nick and Talisha

Nick and Talisha, both in their late-30s, are looking to retire at 60.

This was their financial situation when they came to me:

	Age	Income	Super Balance
Nick	36	$120,000	$130,000
Talisha	34	$100,000	$110,000

By the time they reach retirement, they plan to have paid off their home and be mortgage free, the children will be adults and they see themselves being able to live comfortably on a combined annual income of $100,000 in the first 10 years and $80,000 thereafter. That's a net amount with no tax payable in retirement up to certain limits.

Upon reaching that magic marker point 25 years into the future, based on today's dollar value, their retirement super fund will be sitting at close to $2,800,000, and they are then ready to start withdrawing funds at that predetermined $100,000 per annum. The graph on the next page outlines their financial position until they reach 100 years of age.

They could also benefit from investing into our Portfolio with Private Portfolio Managers and gearing or seeing a buyers agent buying and buying an investment property. The most important point is they must seek advice and spend one day a year on their financial Health. Debt Recycling is a strategy they should consider, this could help pay of the home 10 years earlier.

In retirement they buy a new car or taking a $20,000 trip will really make a difference to their retirement income, but with management and care it's easily achievable to do such things. Their retirement fund is like a bank account and withdrawals can be made; however, you should seek advice as this may affect your retirement.

As their super fund base line diminishes in overall value, then they can also have that diminished value topped up by pension payments to ensure that overall, their net income remains the same.

Retirement Plan

Projections

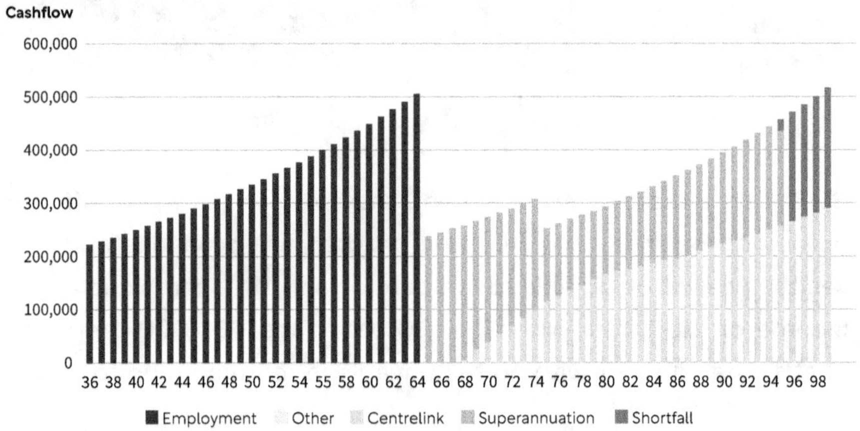

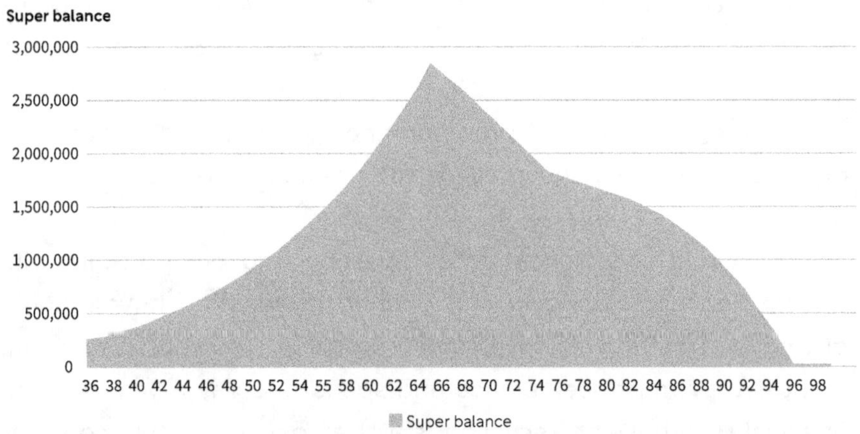

Warren and Victoria

Warren and Victoria are currently enjoying their retirement with a combined super balance of $800,000. They have an income expectation of $75,000 annually. As their super fund diminishes over time, they can rely on their pensions to ensure a sustainable income. They've managed to maintain their lifestyle even as their asset levels decline. It's proof that careful planning pays off!

Warren and Victoria have annuity for $400,000 providing indexed income for life. The annuity has helped Wayne and Vicky achieve their retirement goals and given them the ability to access the pension as only 60% of an annuity counts towards their retirement. The guaranteed extra payments from the government over their lifetime is over $100,000.

Retirement Plan

Projections

Cashflow

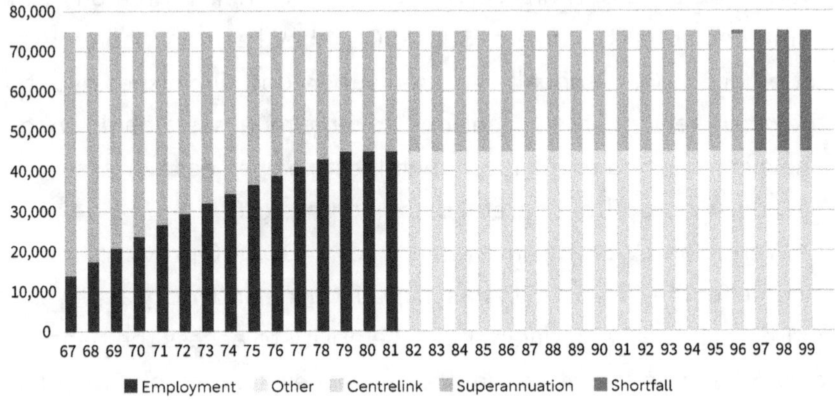

Super balance

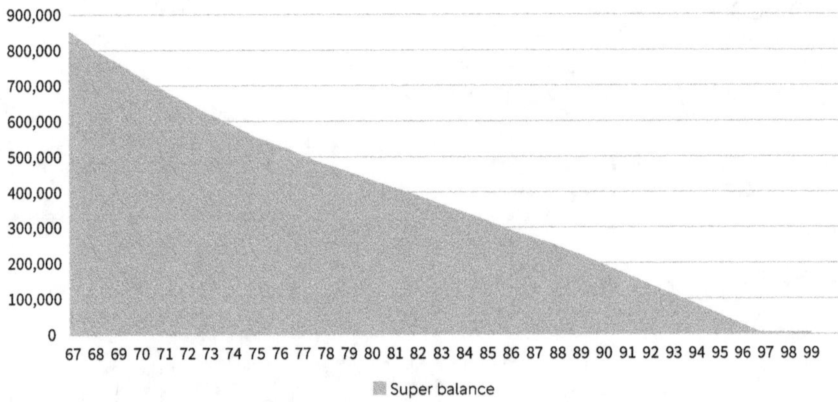

Joe and Matt

Joe and Matt have higher incomes and no dependents. They're aiming for a lifestyle income of $90,000 during early retirement, dropping to $70,000 at age 80. They're on track to achieve a super balance of $2,500,000 by 60 showing that even lofty goals can be within reach with the right planning.

Other considerations for Joe and Matt are that they could use the funds in their offset account to start an investment portfolio. An example of using the $100,000 in the offset account and investing in the Private Portfolio investment account we use can make a difference in retirement, see below investment chart the difference over 20 years is substantial saving $120k in offset versus building a one million portfolio over 20 years

Investment Plan Offset v Investing

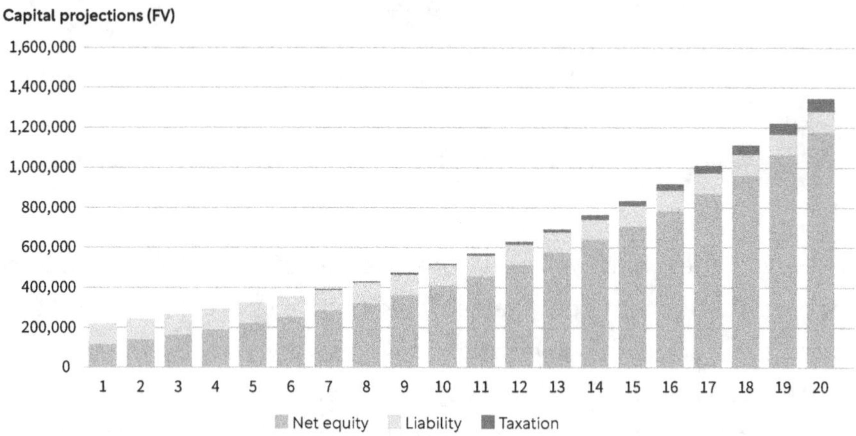

They can also consider the downsizing contribution to boost their super as well as the catch-up contributions. There are so many strategies that can be used, hence the reason for advice. You don't know what you don't know.

Matt and Joe purchased a $700,000 house, renting it out at

$600 per week. Despite additional costs and no immediate income, they're set to see an equity of $1,350,000 in the property after 30 years. It's a long-term strategy that could pay off handsomely! Here's how they did it:

A house purchased at $700K, with additional stamp duty and legal fees, their total investment is $726,775 (please note stamp duty varies from state to state). They rent it out at $600 per week, which is a gross income of $31,200. But their actual costs including allowances of $1,500 for maintenance, $1,200 for insurance and $2,500 rates on top of their mortgage payments of $36,339, (P&I on 6.6% interest terms) means they have to add an extra $5,764 per year to their investment to sustain it. No additional income, but instead a forced saving of approximately $110 per week.

My calculations on borrowing $750,000 to cover all up-front expenses:

	Repayments P&I @ 6% 25 years	Expenses	Income	Cost
Monthly	$4,842	$475	$2,600	$2,717
Yearly	$58,104	$5,700	$31,200	$32,604
Over 25 years	$1,452,678	$142,500	$780,000	$815,178

However, they have an additional bonus of $12,500 per year of depreciation to write off against their income tax each year, and that offsets the additional investment savings very well. By the time the mortgage is paid fully after 30 years, their (inflation-only adjusted) equity in the property is up to $1,350,000. That's not allowing for the fact that the property itself may well outpace the inflation rates over those three decades and be worth considerably more than $1,350,000.

Retirement Plan

Projections

Cashflow

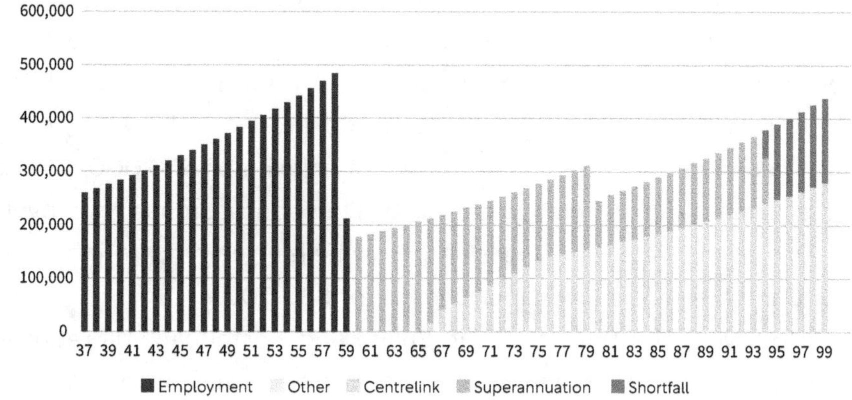

Super balance

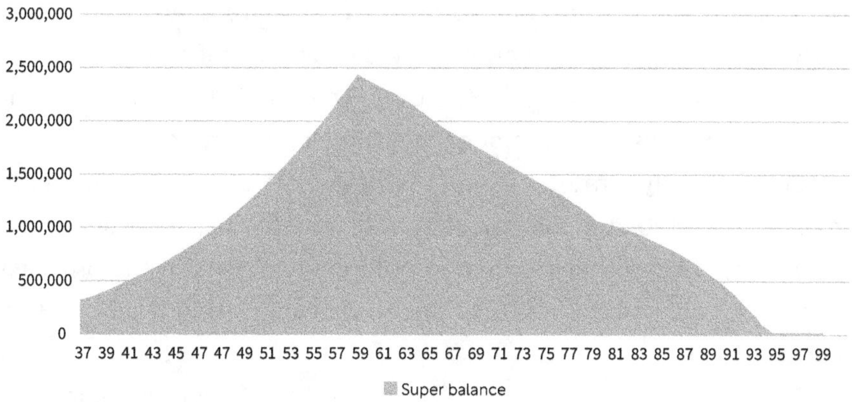

Shane and Kristal

Shane and Kristal, despite low super balances, have planned wisely to retire at 60. Utilising the downsizer contribution and the small business concession, they've mapped out a path to a comfortable lifestyle of $80,000 per year in today's dollars. Here's how they do it:

Shane is a dentist with a low super balance of $50,000. This is due to investing his money into his business and purchasing a lovely house on the water at Hope Island. His wife is an administration assistant and also has a low super balance of $80,000.

However, with the right plan Shane and Kristal can still retire at 60 due to the downsizer contribution. This allows you to put up to $300,000 each into super tax free if you are downsizing your property. They have a 5-bedroom property on the water, which will be a very saleable asset in 17 years. They can also benefit from the small business concession up to $500,000. There are restrictions on this but we can advise them to speak with their accountant.

So, their only strategy is pay the house off, sell the business and make $500,000 net capital gain and transfer this into super, tax free. They will sell their home and potentially downsize the property, and both contribute $300,000 each into super using the downsizer contribution.

This then gives them a very comfortable lifestyle in retirement of $80,000 per annum in today's dollars. This does not include an investment plan such as shares or an investment property, which could also help build even more wealth over the next 17 years before retirement.

They can also consider using the equity in their home to buy an investment property or start a share portfolio. Getting the right advice and strategy is important to their overall goals.

Retirement Plan

Projections

Cashflow

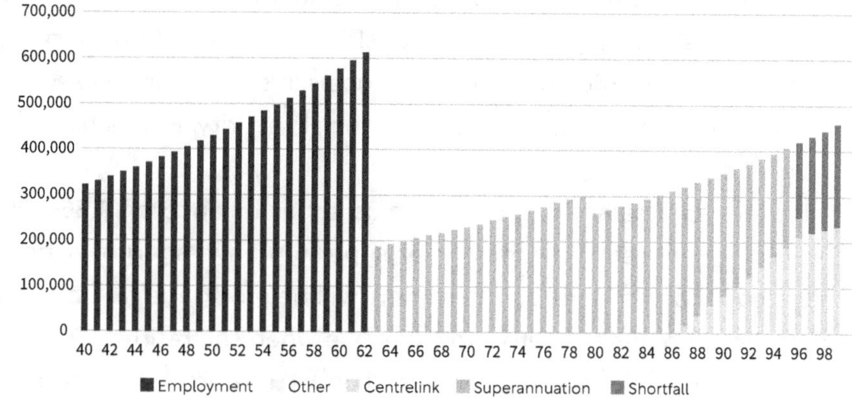

Super balance

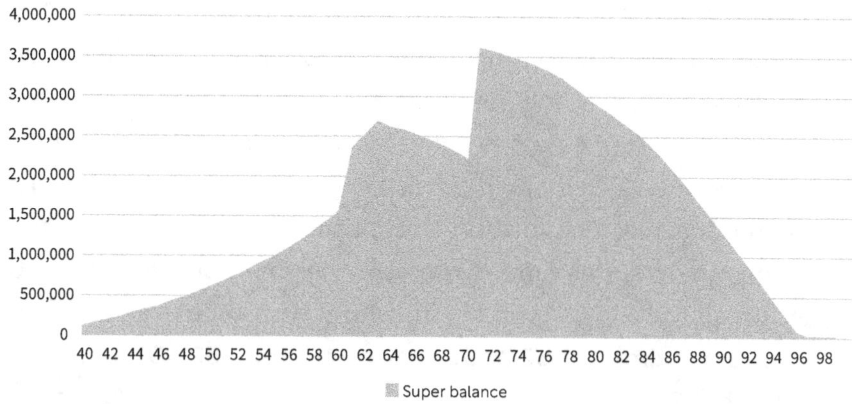

Karen's solo journey

Karen, in her early 40s, seeks a retirement income of $52,000 starting at 65. By maintaining her current position and benefiting from the pension, she's on track to achieve her goals. It's an inspiring example of how solo planners can also find financial security. Here's how she achieves this:

Karen has a salary of $85,000 plus super balance of $136,000. Based on a net return of 6% on her super fund averaged over time, this is easily achievable, and her home will be mortgage free by that time, affording her a comfortable lifestyle when she retires.

Her super will grow to over $1 million by the time she retires at 63. The $52,000 she requires today will be closer to $100,000 in 22 years.

Karen has the option to increase her super fund balance as she pays down her mortgage, or divert the extra funds into an investment property. If she does nothing more than maintain her current position, she is still looking at achieving her current goals. Her pension boost will kick in soon after retirement age of 67, to offset her diminishing super fund. By age 82, her pension benefit will be approximately $28,000 per annum with the balance from her super fund at approximately $24,000 making up the $52,000 until she's well into her 90s.

Retirement Plan

Projections

Cashflow

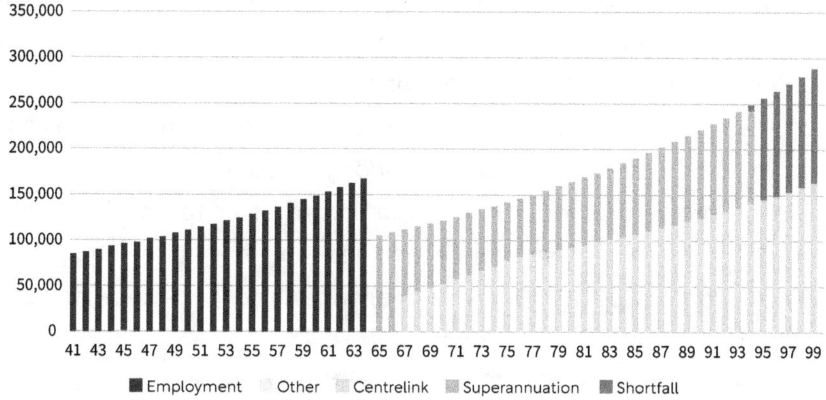

Super balance

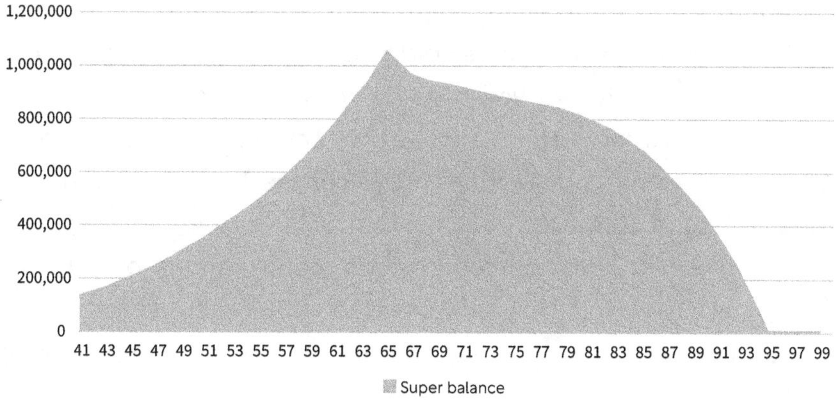

Ant and Emily

They are retiring at 67 and would love to travel in retirement. They would like $140,000 per annum for first 10 years then reduce their travel and receive $100,000 per annum.

They have 2 investment properties, and the plan is to sell these down at retirement and transfer funds into super.

One property should have a net profit after tax of $800,00 i.e. purchase price less sale price and tax and the other should have a net profit of $600,000. The challenge is to get them into super potentially a tax-free environment.

They will use $500,000 to pay of the home loan and invest the balance in super. They should have around $1,300,000 to contribute to super.

The first property may be sold when they turn 67 and the other when they turn 70. As you have up to the age of 75 to get funds into super, this should work nicely. They can put in $120,000 each of non-concessional contributions plus a concessional contribution (tax deductible) of $30,000.

The $120,000 of non-concessional contributions can be done using the 3-year rule that allows you to contribute 3 years' worth of contributions in one go. This is a great way to get lump sums into super. We find this very useful for those who are self-employed and don't have enough in super to retire comfortably.

Ant and Emily want to invest in the stock market and are high growth investors, our fund has averaged over 10% over the long term so I have used 8% in the retirement plan.

Retirement Plan

Projections

Cashflow

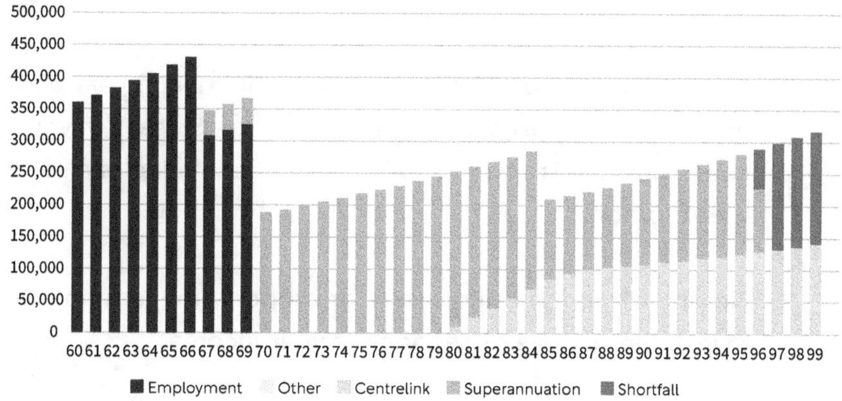

Super balance

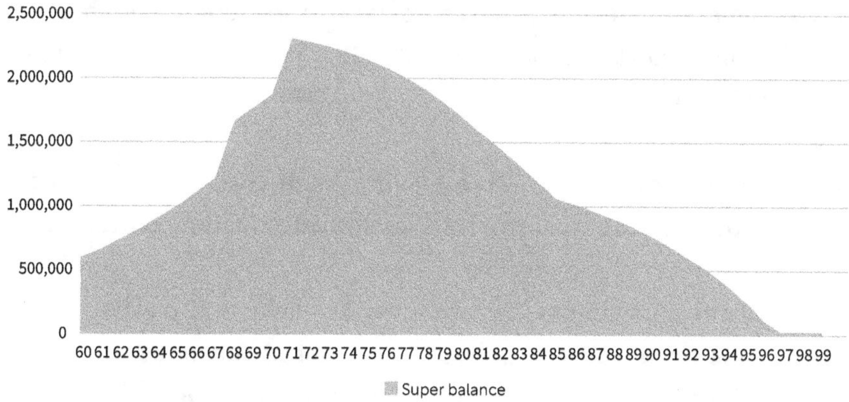

TOP 5 TAX PLANNING TIPS

1. Superannuation of $30K is tax deductible each year and you can use unused contributions up to 5 years if your super balance is under $500k. Salary sacrificing is also a great option.

2. Negative gearing using shares or property the loss on the investment can be offset against your income.

3. Recontribution strategy once you are 60 years old this will help reduce tax payable to your non-dependant family, which can be significant as it is 15% on the taxable portion of Super.

4. Prepay expenses before 30 June each year, i.e. purchasing business-use laptop or business travel or income protection.

5. Timing of selling investments, i.e. have the contract for sale on investment property sold dated July not June. This gives you another 12 months before tax is due.

ADEM'S TOP 10 FINANCIAL PLANNING TIPS FOR AUSTRALIANS

Congratulations on investing in your financial wellbeing by reading this book. These tips have been written for the Australian market, but really you will be able to implement these wherever you live. Hopefully you have been able to relate to the information I have shared and now understand the importance of financial planning.

As a quick summary, these are my top 10 financial tips to inspire you to take action, with a special focus on Australian superannuation and investment options.

1. Dedicate a 'Finance Day'

Take one day a year to focus on your financial health. Review your mortgage, superannuation, insurance and retirement plans. Reach out to your accountant, financial adviser or loan broker for guidance.

2. Start saving early

Save at least 10% of your salary. Thanks to the magic of compound interest, even small amounts can grow substantially over time. And the earlier you start, the greater the return. It is never too late to start.

3. Eliminate high-interest debt

Credit cards and personal loans can be costly. Pay them off as soon as possible to minimise interest.

4. Build an emergency fund

Unexpected expenses happen. Aim to save at least three months' salary to avoid any financial surprises.

5. Invest for the long term

Build wealth by investing in a diversified portfolio of shares and property if you can. Think long-term and quality and let your investments grow.

6. Review your insurance

From life insurance to income cover, ensure you have the right protection for your unique needs.

7. Supercharge your superannuation

Maximise your super by contributing as much as possible and selecting the right investment options. Consider a self-managed super fund (SMSF) if your balance exceeds $300,000. Also consider salary sacrificing or making extra post-tax deductions, which you then may be able to claim in your tax return.

8. Update your will

Life changes, and so should your will. Regularly review it to ensure that your assets will be distributed according to your wishes.

9. Plan for retirement

It's never too early to think about retirement. Start planning now to maintain your lifestyle when the working days are over. At Virtual Financial Advice it is our goal that all out clients have a retirement plan that is reviewed annually.

10. Seek professional advice

A financial planner can keep your financial strategy on track and provide valuable insights tailored to your situation. At Virtual Financial Advice we help people all over Australia reach their goals and plan for the future.

• • •

These tips relate no matter what stage of life you are at. Whether you're just starting on your financial journey or looking to optimise your existing plans, these guidelines can put you on the path to success. Happy Planning!

Endnotes

1 https://www.adviservoice.com.au/2018/02/australians-feeling-better-prepared-retirement-investment-trends-2017-retirement-income-report/

2 https://www.ato.gov.au/Super/self-managed-super-funds/Setting-up

3 https://www.ato.gov.au/forms-and-instructions/superannuation-contributions-splitting

4 https://www.ato.gov.au/individuals-and-families/super-for-individuals-and-families/super/growing-and-keeping-track-of-your-super/caps-limits-and-tax-on-super-contributions/non-concessional-contributions-cap#ato-Aboutthenonconcessionalcontributionscap

5 https://www.ato.gov.au/individuals-and-families/super-for-individuals-and-families/self-managed-super-funds-smsf/smsf-newsroom/highlights-smsf-quarterly-statistical-report-december-2024;

https://www.ato.gov.au/about-ato/research-and-statistics/in-detail/super-statistics/smsf-statistics

6 https://www.ppmfunds.com/

7 https://www.hub24.com.au/

8 https://www.experien.com.au/trauma-insurance-claims-statistics/

9 https://share.google/W6vIc6wFFROfIFGRZ; https://www.abs.gov.au/AUSSTATS/abs@.nsf/Lookup/4392.0Main+Features11995?OpenDocument

10 https://riskinfo.com.au/news/2023/05/29/staggering-number-of-australians-dont-have-life-insurance/

11 https://www.aihw.gov.au/reports/cancer/cancer-data-in-australia/contents/overview

12 https://www.aihw.gov.au/reports/heart-stroke-vascular-diseases/hsvd-facts/contents/all-heart-stroke-and-vascular-disease/coronary-heart-disease

13 https://www.servicesaustralia.gov.au/how-much-jobseeker-payment-you-can-get?context=51411

14 https://www.superannuation.asn.au/consumers/retirement-standard/

15 https://www.superannuation.asn.au/consumers/retirement-standard/

16 www.virtualfinancial.com.au

17 https://www.challenger.com.au/individual/learn/what-is-an-annuity

18 https://www.legacy.challenger.com.au/tools/ff/cgf/#/centrelink

19 https://www.finder.com.au/life-insurance/estate-planning/what-happens-if-i-die-without-a-will-in-nsw

Resources

The below resources are the products that go with our advice, they include Investment platforms and Insurances we mainly use. I encourage you to look at the product disclosure statements (PDS) and get advice before using any products. This is not an extensive list and everyone has a different situation and other investments insurances may be more applicable.

Hub24: www.hub24.com.au

Private Portfolio Managers (PPM): www.ppmfunds.com

Beta Shares: www.betashares.com.au

BT: www.bt.com.au

Shartru Wealth: www.shartruwealth.com.au

Acenda: www.acenda.com.au

Metlife: www.metlife.com.au

Zurich: www.zurich.com.au

Adem Becirevic is a qualified CPA Accountant who specialises in financial advice. With over 25 years of experience helping clients achieve financial freedom now, and in retirement. This is done by using boutique investments and portfolios, and ensuring clients have a retirement and debt recycling plan in place.

Adem uses a holistic approach to wealth including shares and property and gives advise on your personal circumstances. He offers a free 60 minute zoom or teams meeting to see how he can help.

It is his goal to make financial advice affordable for all Australians, and to make a difference.

Virtual Financial Advice
Level 6 200 Adelaide Street, Brisbane
Ph 1300 653 372
www.virtualfinancial.com.au
adem@virtualfinancial.com.au

facebook.com/virtualfinancialgroupaus

linkedin.com/in/virtualfinancial

instagram.com/adembecirevic